The Ancient Goddess

Her Myths, Legends, Sacred Sites and Present Day Revelation

Kathy Jones

Published by
ARIADNE PUBLICATIONS
61 Tor View Avenue, Glastonbury, Somerset,
BA6 8AG, England

Front Cover Painting of Brigit : Foosiya Miller
Back Cover Painting of Shamanka : Foosiya Miller
Cover Design : Lloyd Drew

Illustrations by David Dunger, Diana Griffiths, Foosiya Miller, Kathy Jones,
Marian Elliott, Thalia Brown & Willow Roe
Photographs by Diana Griffiths, Roland Pargeter, Simant Bostock &
Tony Arihanto.
All uncredited photos and illustrations by Kathy Jones.

Typeset and designed by Kathy Jones
Printed by Bookcraft

ISBN 1 872983 23 5

Dedication

To Beloved Britannia, Spinner of the Thread of Life
Weaver of the Web of Connection,
Cutter of the Thread at Death
To She who is Brigit Anna,
The One and the Many
in Brigit's Isles

Acknowledgements

In revising and expanding the Ancient British Goddess I want to acknowledge all the people who have helped create this new edition. Firstly I want to thank the artists who contributed to the original book - Diana Griffiths, Marian Elliott, Thalia Brown, Willow Roe and David Dunger, whose beautiful illustrations are included once again. I also thank the photographers whose images add vibrancy to the text - Diana Griffiths, Roland Pargeter, Simant Bostock and Tony Arihanto.

In this new edition I want to thank Foosiya Miller in particular for her beautiful cover paintings of Brigit and Her Shamanka, and for new illustrations within the book itself. I am grateful to all the Goddess-loving artists who have generously allowed me to include samples of their artwork - Carolyn Hillyer, Jane Brideson, Jill Smith, Katheryn Trenshaw, Monica Sjoo and Phillipa Bowers. I also thank them for their inspiring words. I thank the other contributors for sharing their Goddess experience too - Asphodel Long, Cheryl Straffon, Jana Runnalls, Julie Felix, Lady Olivia Durdin Robertson, Rose Flint and Tyna Redpath.

In creating the book I thank Lloyd Drew for his help in scanning photographs and for his great design for the cover. I thank Mike Jones for the important task of reading and correcting proofs, and for being my Goddess-gifted partner. My love goes always to you and to my lovely Iona and Torquil.

Over the years of my Goddess journey I have been helped by many hundreds of people and mentioning some always leaves out others who should be included, so I ask your forgiveness if you are not named here. You have walked with me through the sacred landscape, you have been with me in ceremony, you have laughed with me, you have been there when I needed you, you have been my friend and I thank you from the bottom of my heart.

My gratitude goes to Tyna Redpath with whom I have had a lot of joy in creating the Glastonbury Goddess Conference over the last seven years. Its a great experience working with you, Tyna. I thank everyone who has contributed to the Glastonbury Goddess Conference in any way as presenters, artists, performers, Melissas and participants. Thank you for helping to create such a joyful, loving Goddess space where we can expand the boundaries of our Goddess experience together. May we long continue together. I thank all the women who over the years have been part of the Conference Ceremonial Group creating and holding the Goddess sacred space, especially the beautiful Aine Carey, the fey queen Rose Flint, the strong Sandra Brant and the gorgeous Sue Oxley.

I thank my friend Collette Barnard, and Chrissie Peters and Ana Morgan of the Isle of Avalon Foundation, who have nurtured and brought to expression many kinds of spiritual teachings, including those of the Goddess, thereby changing people's lives and the world for the better. I thank all the students I have worked with over the years, especially those who have and are taking part in the Priestess of Avalon trainings, which are exciting, challenging and full of Her mystery. As the Orchard of Priestesses grows so we are bringing the presence of the Lady of Avalon back into the world.

I thank Palden Jenkins, a great website designer, who for several years has created a wonderful Goddess in Glastonbury website for me and I thank Geraldine Charles for continuing the work.

I thank all those who are creating the Glastonbury Goddess Temple especially Alison Waite, Ark Redwood, Brian Charles, Carol Morgan, Rachael Clyne, Sally Pullinger and Tegwyn Hyndman. I thank you for having the courage to take up the Goddess flame, letting it shine once again in Her world.

Across the waters in America there are several special women who have helped me to expand my journey with the Goddess, who I want to thank - my friend Edwene Gaines, who is a great teacher and Firewalk instructor; Alene Victoria Balse, a Lady of the Lake who has given me the opportunity to teach in California; Reverend Charlotte Amant whose Goddess light shines in Colorado; Julia McMahon for her generous support; and Leona Graham, my unique and original Goddess-loving friend who has been on the same journey from the beginning. I love you all.

With gratitude, love and blessings
Kathy   Samhain 2001

Contents

Introduction

Welcome to the revised and expanded edition of *The Ancient British Goddess* which was first published in 1991. Over the last ten years our knowledge and experience of the Goddess here in the British Isles has grown and developed beyond measure. The Lady of these islands who was lost in the mists of history is being rediscovered and brought back into the light of day, wearing new clothes, shining with renewed radiance. She is whispering in our ears, appearing in our visions, calling to us across time to remember Her and we are responding. All over Britain thousands of women and men now celebrate the Goddesses of this land in ways which probably haven't happened for a thousand years and more.

When I began my personal quest to find the Goddess over twenty five years ago, Her familiar names in Britain were those of the Greek, Roman and Hindu pantheons. She was Venus, Diana, Artemis, Isis, Kali and Shakti. Britain then was a mainly Christian country and there were no British Goddesses, only names in stories that didn't have the same power as the Goddesses of other lands. But of course Goddess is everywhere and She had to be here too, lost in the mists of our forgetting but here, waiting to be recognised. Like many others I opened my heart to Her and my journey to Her has unfolded. The British Goddesses began to speak to me and I reclaimed them for myself. The first edition of *The Ancient British Goddess* came out of that quest and was one of the first books to name and honour the Goddesses of Britain and Ireland.

Over the last ten years many people have begun to celebrate the presence of our native British Goddesses, as well as those who arrived over the centuries with other races to make a homeland here. Together we are bringing the Goddess alive once again through our worship of Her, through spiritual practice, ceremonies, actions, creative expression, study, writing, artwork, music, dance and in our daily lives. I have expanded the original small book to include information which has

Cover of the first edition

Opposite:Spiralling spider's web, one of the signs and symbols of the Goddess, is visible in Her spring-time Nature

emerged through this experience, as well as looking at the work of modern day Goddess artists, writers and performers and at the Glastonbury Goddess Conference which annually celebrates Her abundant nature.

This book is an evocation of the spirit of the ancient and ever present Goddess of this land. My aim is to describe, reveal and synthesise some of Her many and varied divine qualities. It is not meant to be an exhaustive exposition of all Her manifestations, but is designed to awaken heart feelings for Her in us all. We shall look at some of Her aspects in detail while others will merely be mentioned.

The book is based on mythology, historical texts, the findings of archaeology, experiences at sacred sites, in ceremony and sacred drama and upon memory and imagination. It is not an academic text. There are no footnotes to indicate where every detail has come from although authors are credited where relevant. In particular I salute Robert Graves for his wonderful book *The White Goddess*, Marija Gimbutas for her ground-breaking work in *Language of the Goddess* and *Civilisation of the Goddess*, Caitlin and John Matthews for their many books on Goddesses especially *Ladies of the Lake*, and Michael Dames for his Goddess inspired views of landscape in *The Avebury Cycle* and *Silbury Treasure*. I applaud all the modern day priest/esses, poets, artists, musicians and writers who are bringing Her alive once again.

This book is about a living Goddess honoured in the past and returning to our consciousness now in new forms. My interest is in bringing the Goddess alive in the present day and that means being open to receiving Her inspiration here and now. So I have allowed my imagination to flow.

In this magical journey through the spiritual world of the Goddess, I take Brigit's Isles - the Goddess name for the British Isles, (say it quickly enough and it sounds the same), to be an intimately connected geographical and mythic whole, which includes all of England, Wales, Scotland and Ireland. This is not a political territorial claim by the British over Irish and other cultures, but a return to the rightful allegiance of all these lands to Brigit, whose name originally meant Goddess. Information is gleaned about our native Goddesses from wherever it is available.

Brigit's Isles have ancient ties to the continent of Europe being physically connected to it for hundreds of thousands of years. Then there was a universal belief in the power of the Goddess dating from the earliest times, before land had become territory, owned by human beings. Then the Earth was known to be Her body, ruled by Her nature and the

The beautiful golden Lammas Goddess made by Lucy Lepchani for the first Glastonbury Goddess Conference in 1996

Source of all life. During the last Ice Age Brigit's Isles were joined to Europe, separating in about 9,000 BCE (Before the Common Era), when the seas rose and flowed between the separated lands.

Our journey takes us from the natural world of our early palaeolithic ancestors through the sacred landscapes of the neolithic or new stone age, when mounds, long barrows, standing stones and stone circles were erected between the 6th and 3rd millennia BCE. We will draw threads of connection between our neolithic forebears who loved the Goddess and the legends of the warrior Kelts. We will bring these stories into the present day gathering inspiration and knowledge on the way as we explore the work of modern day Goddess-loving creative women.

The Ancient British Goddess

In ancient Britain the Goddess was the One who expressed Herself through the Many. She was the great Void, the Beginning of all things. She was the Source of Life, the Creatrix, Continuer and Destroyer of all that exists. She was the Matrix, the Great Mother, Spinner of the Thread of Life and Destiny, Weaver of the Web of Continuity and Cutter of the Thread at death. All souls were born from Her sacred Womb, lived for a span upon Her Body the Earth , then returned to Her Tomb/Womb at death. She was Mother of the Stars in the Heavens and of all Nature. She was the Tree of Life.

She was the Maiden, the Mother and the Crone; the Virgin, the Lover and the Whore. The Holy Grail of Immortality, the Chalice of Love and the Cauldron of Transformation were all in Her keeping, reflecting Her Triple nature. She was the Three, Nine and Nineteen Sisters, Ladies, Maidens, Mothers, Faerie Queens, Crones or Hags, who expressed themselves through the fourfold cycle of Her seasons.

Opposite: Our Mother Nature by Marian Elliott

The spinning circle of the Nine Ladies of Stanton in Peak in Derbyshire

1

Nothing has changed, it is all still true! She lives now, today, here in our land!

In legend and landscape She has many Names

In Ireland She is Aibhinn, Ailech the White, Ailinn, Aine, Almu, An, Anny, Ana, Anu, Anu-Dana, Aoibheall, Artha, Badbh, Banbha, Beansidhe, Blanaidd, Bo, Boand, Breacha, Brid, Brighde, Brigit, Buanann, Cailleach Bheare, Carman, Cron, Cymeidi Cymeinfoll, Dana, Danu, Domnu, Eadon, Eblinne, Echtga, Eithne, Erin, Eriu, Etain, Fand, Fedelm, Flidas, Fodhla, Garbh Ogh, Grainne, Grian, Hag of Bheara, Kessair, Kersair, Kele, Liban, Life, Macha, Maeve, Lady Mary, Medb, Morrighan, Niamh of the Golden Hair, Queen of the Sidhe, Sadb the Deer Mother, Sheela na Gig, Sinnann, Tailtiu, Tara, Tea and the Woman with the Silver Branch.

In Wales She is Arianrhod of the Silver Wheel, Blodeuwedd the Flower Maiden and Owl, Branwen, Cordelia, Creiddylad, Creidne, Creirwy, Elen, Fflur, Flower Maiden, Ganieda, Gwenddydd, triple Gwenhwyfar (triple White Phantom), Helen, Iris, Keridwen, Lady of Llyn y Fan Fach, Maumau, Meredith, Mona, Morfydd, Olwen of the White Track, Rhiannon, Sheela na Gig, White Sow and Winifride.

In Scotland She is Bera, Bride, Cailleach Dubh (Dark Old Woman), Cailleach na Mointeach (of the moors), Cailleach na Montaigne (of the mountain), Cale, Car, Carline, Io, Ioua the Moon, Mag Moullach, Scathach, Scota and Scotia.

In England She is Agnes, Alba, Albina, Ambrosia, Amma, Ana, Anna, Angnes, Anna Favina, Annis, Apple Woman, Argante, Ariadne, Artha, Black Annis, Black Maiden, Blue Hag, Bona Dea, Bree, Breeshey, Brigantia, Britannia, Cardea, Cat Annis, Cliton, Countess of the Fountain, Coventina, Crone, Dame Ragnell, Dana, Dark Mother, Dea Matronae, Dea Nutrix, Diana, Dindraine, Elaine, Elen of the Trackways, Enid, Eostre, Epona, Etain, Faery Queen, Flora, Fortuna, Giantess, Gliten, Glitonea, Goda, Graine, Green Lady, Green Woman, Guinevere, Hag, Harvest May, Helen, Hoeur, Igraine, Isis, Ker, Kernel, Kerhiannon, Koeur, Kundri, Lady Bertilak, Lady of Avalon, Lady of the Fountain, Lady of the Lake, Ma, Mab, Madron, Maia, Maiden of the Cart, Maid Marian, Mam, Mary, Madron, Mazoe, Modron, Morgaine, Morg-Ana, Morgen la Fey,

Opposite: Painting - The Tree of Life by Foosiya Miller

2

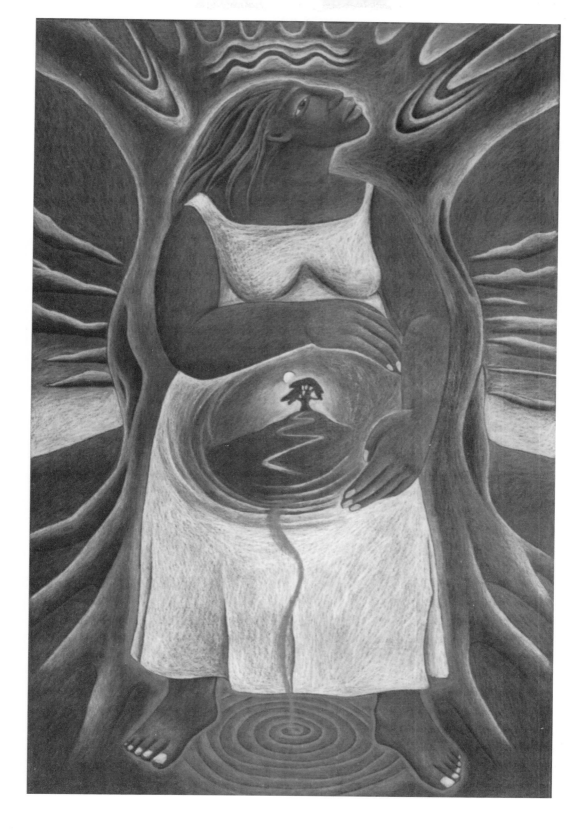

"*Cornwall - Sacred Land of the Goddess*", painting by Monica Sjoo, showing the Cheese Ring, the Hurlers, Quoit and the Mothers.

Moronoe, the Mothers, Nimue, Nine Maidens, Nine Morgens, Nine Sisters, Nine Witches of Gloucester, Oestre, Old Wife, Old Woman, Our Lady of Glastonbury, Our Lady of Walsingham, Phaedria, Pomona, Queen of Elfame, Queen of Fate, Queen of the May, Queen of the Wasteland, Raven Queen, Regan, Rigantona (Great Queen), Sabrina, Sovereignty, Spring Queen, Sulis Minerva, Swan Maiden, Thetis, Thitis, Tree of Life, Tyronoe, Ur, Ursel, Vivienne, Verbeia, Venus, Washer at the Ford, White Doe, White Lady, Wise Woman of Wookey Hole.

Hail to you, Brigit Anna
Hail Great Queen of Brigit's Isles
Hail Sovereignty, Our Lady Britannia
Hail Goddess of ten thousand names
May you be honoured and adored forever !

(Sources for the names of Goddesses include *Complete Irish Mythology* by Lady Gregory, *Iona* by Fiona Macleod, *The Golden Key and the Green Life* by Elizabeth Sutherland, *Ladies of the Lake* by Caitlin and John Matthews, *The Mabinogion* translated by Lady Charlotte Guest, *The Modern Antiquarian* by Julian Cope, *Ortho Nan Gaidheal* by Alexander Carmichael, *The Serpent and the Goddess* by Mary Condren, *The Silver Branch Cards* by Nicholas Mann, *The Sun and the Serpent by Hamish Miller and Paul Broadhurst, *Trioedd Ynys Prydein*, edited by Rachel Bromwich, *The White Goddess* by Robert Graves.)

The Early Goddess Reigned Alone

For the long ages of the palaeolithic era before 30,000BCE, the Goddess reigned alone. She was the Origin, the Virgin Void out of which She was Self-created. She was present in all forms of life. Her arching Body was the star-filled Sky. She was the Sun, the Moon and the Stars and the Space between. She was Mother Nature, Mistress of the animals and the plants. The Earth was Her Body. The rivers and oceans were Her blood and life fluids. The plants, trees and vegetation were Her hair.

She was the Mother of Time. In ancient Britain the pattern of life was determined by the cycle of Her seasons. Through the turning of the year Her body was visibly transformed from the fresh green Maiden, to the vibrant Lover, to the radiant Mother and the slowly dying Crone. Through the aeons this cycle of transformation repeated itself, interrupted only by the Ice Ages in which the British Isles were completely covered in glaciers and sheets of ice.

Below left: the fresh Green Maiden appears in the sprouting buds Below right: the Vibrant Lover shows Her colours as the trees unfurl their new leaves

Above left: Thousands of leaves grow on the Radiant Mother tree. Above right: The slowly Dying Crone loses her leaves and exposes her bones

Images of the Goddess as Woman

Images of the Goddess in a woman's form first appear in Europe in the Upper Paleolithic era, from 30-20,000 BCE. They show different aspects of the Goddess's abundant nature as expressed in women's inherent capability to carry and give birth to children, and to feed them for the first years of life from the milk in their breasts. These figures are nearly always naked and the head and face are often unfeatured, but sometimes show markings of hairstyles or hats.

Some figurines have rounded fertile bodies with large breasts full of milk, the Goddess's hands resting upon Her pregnant life-giving womb. In others She is slim-shouldered with hands on Her breasts and bulging thighs and visible genitals. Sometimes She is reddened with ochre, faint traces still showing on the images. In Her death aspect She is stiff and white, carved in bone and chalk. Few male figures have been found dating from these early times.

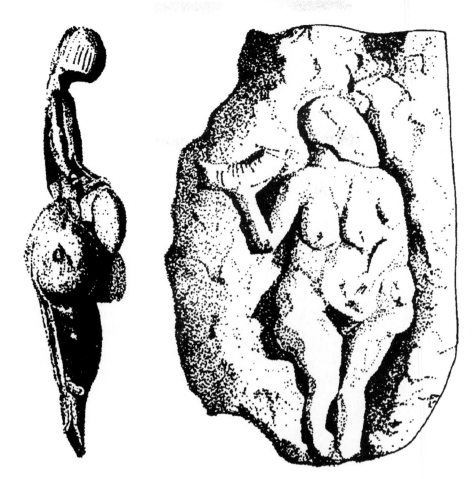

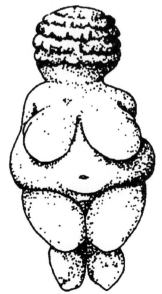

Early European Goddess images:
Above left, the Venus of Lespugue dating from 20,000BCE - the fertile Maiden Goddess with emphasised hips, thighs and buttocks.
Above right, the Venus of Laussel from the Dordogne in France dating from 25,000BCE - the Mother Goddess with her hand resting on her protruding pregnant belly. She holds a bison horn in one hand which has 13 lunar notches. She is still stained with red ochre.
Right, the Venus of Willendorf dating from 30,000BCE. The Fruitful Mother Goddess who has just given birth. Her hands rest on Her full milky breasts. She wears a woven hat or headdress.

The Goddess and the God

After aeons of sole creation, for unknown reasons, except maybe the desire of Her daughters to share Her love, the Goddess sought a mate, a God to play with, to make love to, with whom She could bear human children with divine souls. She was the radiant Sun whose light and warmth gave life to the earth. He was the silver Moon, who reflected Her light. Each lunar cycle His body would slowly swell to fullness and He would make love to the Sun in the darkness beneath the horizon. His fullness expended He would then shrink and disappear into the days of the dark Moon to await regeneration. He was the father of all human children and women began their monthly bleeding, their moontime, after making love to the Moon God.

The Sun Goddess sinks towards the west where she and the Moon God make love in the darkness beneath the horizon

Wind blows through the willow trees whispering secrets to those with ears to hear

Early gatherer/hunter peoples in Britain as elsewhere lived a nomadic lifestyle, travelling through defined circuits of territory, which they knew intimately. For them the Goddess and the God were visible in the landscape, in the mountains and rivers, in the wind, rain and sunshine, in the forces of Nature. They were also to be found in the plants and the trees which covered the land and sustained their lives and in the animals who shared the same territory.

Ancient British Goddess

In the colder regions of the world, which included Britain for much of the paleolithic and mesolithic eras, the bodies of animals were essential to the lives of early nomadic people. They provided food, protein; skins and guts for clothing, protection and warmth; horns, bones, feathers, teeth and hooves for tools, for decoration and ritual purposes. The animals were viewed as Divine Creatures.

Beautiful cave paintings of many kinds of animals have been found in central and southern France, Spain and Portugal dating from between 30,000-10,000 BCE. The famous cave paintings of Lascaux in France date from 15,000 BCE. Fabulous images of animals are found deep inside caves and must have been painted by the light of flickering oil lamps. Sometimes they overlook an abyss to even lower levels, suggesting that they were offerings to the Dark Earth Mother. Small ochred handprints suggest that the painters of these images were probably women. No such equivalents have been found in Britain which during this time was in the grip of an Ice Age.

The Arrival of the Neolithic Era

The huge ice sheet of the last Ice Age began to retreat northwards from the British Isles from about 9,000 BCE onwards. The earth slowly warmed and Neolithic or New Stone Age culture began to flourish in Britain from around 4,500 BCE. Sea levels were much lower than they are now as sea-water was locked up in huge polar icecaps. Southern Britain had a Mediterranean climate while Northern Scotland was like southern Britain is now. In 1150 BCE a volcanic explosion in Iceland produced huge quantities of dust in the atmosphere, creating a mini Ice Age in Britain. The large widespread population retreated southwards.

Neolithic culture with its large ritual architecture of mounds, barrows and standing stones was found all over the world, dating from approximately 8,000 BCE onwards. There is much speculation by archaeologists and historians as to its origins in the area of the Fertile Crescent covering modern day Iraq, Iran, Turkey, Israel, Jordan and Lebanon. It is here that domestic varieties of grains with their increased flour content are first believed to have been cultivated, harvested, ground into flour, baked into bread, stored for winter, etc.. These developments allowed people to settle and live in one place, rather than having to move seasonally in search of food.

Evidence of the growing and grinding of grain is seen earlier in the grindstones found in Egypt, dating from 15,000 BCE. There was also a parallel development in the cultivation of grain in the Far East, from the same time as in the Near East.

Neolithic culture with its megalithic architecture followed from this discovery of the secrets of the grain and is believed to have slowly diffused outwards from the Fertile Crescent in the four directions by land and sea. Some of its most outstanding architectural remains are to be found in the remaining megalithic sites of Brigit's Isles and Western Europe, particularly in Brittany in France, which has always had close connections to Brigit's Isles.

Neolithic ritual mound or passage grave aligned ESE and surrounded by a ring of stones at Kercado in Brittany dating from 4675BCE

These megalithic remains are part of a recognisable ritual landscape, in which stone and earth monuments were placed within the context of surrounding hills and valleys, rivers and streams. This ability to look at landscape as a whole is one of the predominant features of neolithic society. The people of those times knew about the natural rhythms of Mother Earth. They had knowledge of the movements of the stars. They knew how to correctly position stones and mounds within

Castlerigg stone circle, Cumbria, is beautifully placed in the centre of a cauldron of hills.

Carved kerb stone from the great ritual mound at Knowth in the Boyne Valley in Eire.

the landscape in order to maintain the balance and harmony of their Mother's Body. They knew how to communicate with Star beings. They knew much that we have forgotten.

As Marija Gimbutas showed through her inspired archaeological research the attributes of the neolithic Goddess are expressed in a symbolic language found carved on standing stones and inside ritual mounds which date in Britain from 4,500 BCE onwards, the beginning of the neolithic era.

According to Marija the main theme of this symbolism is the mystery of birth and death and the renewal of life, not just human life but all life on earth. Symbols and images cluster around the Goddess as Giver of Life and Wielder of Death and around the Earth Mother, the Fertility Goddess, young and old, who rises and dies with the plant life. Particular patterns are associated with different Goddesses. For example chevrons and Vs are associated with the Bird Goddess whose concern is life creation and regeneration. Zigzags represent water and female moisture. Snakes are a symbol of life energy often emerging from water. Concentric rings represent the all-seeing eyes of the Goddess.

There are symbols which represent cyclical, not linear, mythical time, manifesting in dynamic swirling motions, whirling and twisting spirals, winding and coiling snakes, circles, crescents, horns, sprouting seeds and shoots. For further information please read the wonderful *Language of the Goddess* by Marija Gimbutas.

Above left: a recentl;y excavated carved stone from inside the ritual mound at Knowth in the Boyne Valley.
Above right: Long Meg with its curved spirals is to be found with Her Sisters - a large ring of standing stones - near Penrith in Cumbria

13

Within the standing stones of Callanish on the Isle of Lewis, northwest Scotland, the hidden form of the ancient Goddess and our neolithic Ancestors, can be seen.

There are few carved images or figurines of the Goddess from this time in Britain although as many people have noticed there are numerous figures and faces, human, divine and animal in the forms and shapes of the megalithic stones which are found all over Brigit's Isles from Callanish in the northwest Scotland to Avebury in Wiltshire.

Terence Meaden has shown in his book *The Secrets of the Avebury Stones* that many of the standing stones at Avebury contain the faces and forms of our ancestors, of the Goddess and Gods of ancient times which are highlighted through the day as the sun travels across the sky.

Opposite page: Whale stone from the Avenue at Avebury. Viewed from the other side this stone looks like a hooded old woman

Prominent stone head in the Avebury circle decorated with flower wreath made by June Peel

Ancient British Goddess

One of the earliest figurines of the Goddess in Brigit's Isles was found preserved in the peat of the Somerset Levels. She dates from 3250 BCE and is 6" tall and carved out of ash wood. Although claimed by archaeologists to be a hermaphrodite god doll, She has typical large breasts and a lower protusion, which is on her left side, like a leg rather than in any central phallic position. She was found beneath the Bell Track, one of the ancient wooden trackways which once crisscrossed the watery Levels, where nomadic people fished and hunted throughout the mesolithic and neolithic eras. Perhaps she is the earliest representation of the Lady of the Lake.

Goddess found in the peat of the Somerset levels from c3250BCE

In early European shrines from 8,000 BCE onwards the Goddess is often represented in figurines, carvings and wall paintings as being part animal and part human-divine. She is the Snake Goddess with a woman's body and snake-like limbs, hair and head. She is the Bird Woman with the body of a woman and the face, feet and wings of a bird or the body of a bird and the face of the woman. She is the Sacred Sow, Cow, Fish, Frog, Dog, Mother Bear and Deer. The qualities of the animals were Her qualities. The shamanka (woman shaman) would invoke the powers of the Goddess by decorating her body with pigments, skins and feathers, wearing headdresses made from animal heads or Her horns.

Snake Goddess from Kato Ierapetera, Krete 6000BCE

The early God was associated with hunting and the animals and like the Goddess also took His forms from the animal world. Shamans identified with the God's power, dressing in feathers, horns and animal skins. This was part of an ancient tradition and some cave paintings show men wearing animal skins, heads and horns.

The early Gods were often horned animals - the Sacred Bull, Ram, Goat, Elk, Buffalo and Bison. There was the Stag God Kernunnos represented on the Gundestrop Cauldron with stag horns on his head. He is consort to the Grain Goddess Ker, who is also a Horned One. Horns are magical antennae connecting the head to the stars. As image they represent both divine Masculine potency and the fallopian tubes and womb of the Goddess.

In Britain certain animals have been revered from the earliest times as divine, playing magical roles in stories of transformation. They include the Salmon of Wisdom, the Sea Eagle, the Wren, Green Woodpecker, Owl, Ousel, Frog or Toad, Hare, Crow and Raven. These animals are totems/magical spirit creatures or Goddesses and Gods depending on one's point of view.

Ancient British Goddess

In later European mythology Goddesses and Gods were often represented as being part human, part animal and part divine. They are the Swan Maidens and Swan Princes who live for a time as human beings and then for a time as swans. Brigit, Madron, Hathor and Kali are all both Sacred Cows and Goddesses; the centaur Chiron was divine human and horse; Rhiannon is Goddess and White Mare; Pan is the Goat and Godman; Keridwen is woman and divine Sow; Asterion the Minotaur was human and divine Bull; the Oannes of Sumer and the Nommo were human/god and Dolphin or Fish.

The "Wizard" of Les Trois Freres, Ariege, 13,000BCE

The fish-tailed Oannes who brought civilisation to the Babylonians from Sirius, carved on gemstones, in the British Museum.

Goddess and God were worshipped together and separately in the cycle of the Seasons of the Sun and the Moon. Living closely in Her nature the spirals of Divine Life were experienced by all human beings, who knew that their lives depended upon divine Grace. The partnership between Goddess and God could be seen in the round of nature. The marriage between Goddess and God was celebrated annually with great jubilation. Women were recognised as having direct access to the divine through their innate ability to bear children, to create Life from within their own bodies. They were the planters of grain, fertilising the earth with their menstrual moon blood. Men were Guardians of Nature.

With the arrival of patriarchal religions the seasonal sacrifice of the God in human and animal form became the norm. His death blood was spilt upon the Earth in the mistaken belief that like life-giving menstrual blood it too would bring fertility to the land and the people. The God's chosen representative on earth was given in marriage to the Queen of the land. For the duration of his royal marriage to the Goddess, the Chosen One was given all his heart desired. When his time had passed he was killed. These ritual deaths reflected the demise of the Goddess who seeks no blood sacrifice, only the honouring of the holy blood of the Womb and of life.

Ancient British Goddess

The neolithic Goddess was associated with cultural creativity in all its aspects particularly those traditionally associated with women - planting, gathering and harvesting, bread baking, making fire and shelters, carding, spinning, weaving, sewing, cookery, teaching, poetry, arts, crafts and healing. Small statues of the Goddess have been found many times in granaries and under bread kilns and in other relevant places throughout ancient Europe.

In Legends and Landscape

The earliest stories which mention the Goddess in Britain were first written down around the turn of the second millennium CE (Common Era). They include legends retained from an ages-old oral tradition in which storytellers, bards and ollaves remembered, spoke and sang the long stories of their ancestors, the mythic divine beings who had created the land and lived upon it. These tales were written down by monks living in all male monasteries, who were themselves devoted to One Male Christian God. Their retelling of the lives of the pantheon of early British and Irish Goddesses and Gods was inevitably distorted.

These stories belong to the Kelts whose culture arose in Brigit's Isles in approximately 500 BCE spreading here from Germany and Central Europe, almost two thousand years after neolithic culture had disappeared. The Kelts were followed by the Romans developing a widespread influential Romano-Keltic culture which lasted for several hundred years. With the fall of the Roman Empire, the following Dark Ages and invasions by Norse and Saxon peoples from the north and east, Keltic culture was gradually pushed to the western land margins where it was retained as it still is today, in the faraway places of Cornwall, Wales, Ireland and Scotland. The first stories of the early peoples of Brigit's Isles are therefore to be found in Irish and Welsh mythology. In our quest to find the ancient British Goddess we can expand their essence to include all of Brigit's Isles.

On the whole these early stories are tales of Keltic heroes and glorify the masculine ideals of war and conquest. They also contain faint glimmers of an earlier, more peaceful age in Brigit's Isles, perhaps during the neolithic, a time in which the Goddess was revered. These legends have to be sifted with a keen eye in order to find clues to the beliefs of our neolithic forebears about the ancient Goddess on whom their lives depended.

The Fomoire
People of Domnu of the Ocean

The first peoples who lived in Brigit's Isles are recorded in the 11th century Irish Book of Invasions as the Fomoire, who lived in Ireland. They were an aboriginal race who worshipped the Goddess Domnu, whose name meant Abyss or the Deep Sea. They were said to be the offspring of Chaos and Old Night. In legend the Fomoire are described as being frightening Giants, mostly women of extremely ugly appearance, with single arms, legs and eyes. One of them called Lot had four eyes in her back and her bloated lips were in her breasts. This could also be a description of some neolithic Goddess carvings.

The Fomoire were originally associated with the sea and the isles of immortality. Fomoire means under sea. They were sea phantoms like the Nommo of the Dogon people of Mali or the Oannes of Sumer, who were part divine/human and part fishlike creatures believed to originate from Sirius. The Fomoire liked to live close to their watery origins. In folklore their stories continue in the tales of Mermaids and Mermen, of Selchies or seal women, who can change from their animal to human forms, often marrying mortal men and having children before returning to the sea. The Fomoire later became connected to the underground sidhe (pronounced *shee*), magic neolithic mound dwellings, to caves and hollow hills beside the sea. Here they and the Goddess Domnu may still be contacted.

Goddess figurine with 12 necklaces, eyes and breasts from central Turkey, early 3rd millennium BCE

Queen Medh's Grave is a large burial mound on top of the royal mountain, Knocknarea, overlooking the sea at Sligo in Eire. Many smaller burial mounds, cairns and standing stones are aligned to this magical sidhe where Queen Medh & Domnu may be contacted.

The People of Kessair, Kersair, of Ker the Grain Goddess

The first recorded immigrants to Ireland and Brigit's Isles were the Race of Kessair, Cessair or Kersair (see the later section on the Goddess Ker). Kersair was said to be a daughter of Bith the Cosmos, and She was also connected to the Sea, in particular to the waters of the Flood - the great deluge recorded in many ancestral traditions. Her consort is the Sea God Finntan, who is the son of the Ocean Bochna.

Kersair is related to the Grain Goddess Ker (also known as Koeur, Kore, Kale, Cor and Car) and it was probably these people, who are recorded as being mainly women, who first brought the secrets of the Grain across the sea from Europe to Brigit's Isles. The women of Kersair sowed the new strains of wheat they brought with them in clearings in the forests and on the sea coasts and the once nomadic gatherer/hunter people began to settle on the land. The neolithic revolution had begun in Brigit's Isles.

Kessair is sometimes equated with the Goddess Banbha who is mentioned in a lost early manuscript as being there before the Flood. Banbha however is identified not with the sea, but with the land which sank beneath the Flood and later re-emerged from the sea. Ireland is known as the island of Banbha of the women.

The People of Artha, the Great She Bear

Several hundred years later the Race of Partholon came to Ireland. I name these people as followers of Artha (out of P(artha)lon), who is the Great She Bear of the heavens. The people of Parthalon were said to be a group of 24 women and 24 men, dedicated it seems to equality between the sexes, and to the Bear Mother who according to ancient belief was the First Mother who gave birth to all human beings. This ancient Bear Mother was worshipped from mesolithic times throughout Europe and Eurasia. She is connected to the Earth Mother Ertha or Eortha, to Ars, Artio and Artemis Callisto also a Bear Mother. Artha is the true Mother of the British hero/king Arthur, whose name comes from Art Vawr meaning *Heavenly Bear*. The race of Partholon arrived in Ireland at Beltane, which has long been known as the festival of the fertile Goddess of Love (see Rhiannon).

According to legend the people of Artha lived peacefully in Ireland for five thousand years, having children, clearing the land, creating lakes and rivers, and later introducing the plough and agriculture. Their arrival brought neolithic culture fully into Brigit's Isles. They were craftspeople who in Ireland built the great mounds in the Boyne valley at Brugh na Boinne. In England and Wales, they built huge long barrows where the ancestors were honoured and where personal and communal ceremonies were performed.

As well as being descendants of Artha the Race of Partholon honoured the Sun Mother, Grainne. They oriented the openings of their great ritual mounds to the movements of the sun at particular times of the year and to the rising full moon. Passages were aligned towards sunrise or sunset at the Winter and Summer Solstices, the Spring and Autumn Equinoxes. Their Goddess was the regenerating Sun whose fiery rays at Winter Solstice signalled the promised return of light and life in the depths of winter. They decorated the stones inside and surrounding their ritual sites with circles, spirals, eyes and suns, all signs

The great reconstructed mound of New Grange at Brugh na Boinne in Ireland

21

of the Goddess (see *Language of the Goddess* by Marija Gimbutas). Cup marks show where they made ritual offerings and mixed the pigments used to colour the carvings. They worshipped the Great Bear they could see in the heavens above them and the Sun Goddess of Love and Regeneration.

At Brugh na Boinne there are three great mounds of New Grange, Knowth and Dowth which contain some of the best examples of megalithic Goddess artwork in the world. After its rediscovery in the last century New Grange was reconstructed as the archeologists at that time thought it might have originally looked. They found large quantities of white quartz and placed it in the facia of the mound. It was later realised that white quartz is a feature of many neolithic sites and was more likely laid as a pavement in front of the entrance to the mound to reflect light into the mound.

New Grange is a passage tomb with a sloping 19 metre passage lined with standing stones leading into a cruciform burial chamber. The corbelled roof of the burial chamber is 6 metres high and still waterproof after 5,000 years. Within the chamber there is beautiful artwork and large decorated stone basins. One of the most amazing features of New Grange is the small opening above the entrance. At dawn on the morning of winter solstice a narrow shaft of sunlight penetrates the passage creeping slowly up the slope to the very back of the chamber lighting up the carvings. An awesome sight to see.

Opposite: the entrance to Brugh na Boinne is aligned to the rising sun at the Winter Solstice. Note the light box above the entrance

The famous triple Goddess spiral carved on the entrance stone at New Grange and repeated inside the chamber.

The largest passage grave in the Boinne Valley is at Knowth. The main mound has two separate passages which are oriented to the rising and setting sun at the Spring and Autumn Equinoxes, and which lead to two separate chambers. Knowth contains the largest collection of Goddess artwork in one place anywhere in the neolithic world. The mound itself is not open to the public but the site can be visited and the beautifully decorated kerb stones can be seen. Eighteen smaller passage tombs and ritual mounds encircle the main mound.

The great mound at Knowth with two satellite mounds

One of the most interesting features of many early neolithic sites is their particular orientation to the rays of the Sun Mother. The actual moment that was celebrated was the entry of rays of light into a dark inner womb chamber. The entry of light obviously signalled the moment of renewal and rebirth for the souls of the dead and for the living. In the late neolithic this feature changed. A tall phallic stone was then placed in front of the entrance to the mound so that instead of light entering the mound it was the shadow cast by the stone which entered the mound. This was the beginning of patriarchal phallic culture and was later applied to stone circles as well as burial mounds. Stonehenge in England is one such example where the original fertilising force was light, later replaced by the shadow cast by an outlying stone.

The Tuatha De Danaan
People of the Goddess Danu

The next great recorded arrival in Brigit's Isles was that of the Tuatha de Danaan, the people of the Goddess Dana, who is also known as Danu, Anu, Anu Dana, Ana, Aine (pronounced Anya), Anna and Amma. She is Mother of all the Gods and some say She is also Domnu, Goddess of the Fomoire. She is BuAnnan the Good Mother and the first of the three Fates of Ana, Badbh and Macha, together known as the Morrigan or Great Queen. Her people were said to have arrived from the sky, landing on a mountain in Ireland.

Goddess Dana was masculinised in later Welsh mythology to become Don and the stories of the Tuatha de Danaan are equated with those of the People of Don in the parallel Welsh mythological cycle of

Stone circles built perhaps by the Tuatha de Danaan
Below left: Some of the 80 stones of the Rollright stone circle in Oxfordshire
Below right: Stone from the circle in the central henge at Avebury which connect the earth and the underground waters to the starry heavens.

the Mabinogion. This long saga begins with the tale of the demise of the Welsh Goddess Rhi-Ann-on who is also known as Rigantona - Great Queen. In British myth the People of Don are the El or Elves, the Shining Ones who retreated into the forests long, long ago. In Saxon tales in England Ana in her role as Fate was known as Black Annis, Annis the Blue Hag or Cat Annis. She is also Ana Our Mother, MorgAna the Virgin/Crone and Anna the Grand Mother Goddess. Her name was found throughout the ancient Goddess world where she was Anna-Nin, Ana-hita, Di-Ana, Ari-An-dne and In-Anna.

The Tuatha de Danaan brought the culmination of neolithic evolution, building great outdoor temples of standing stones, which still survive to this day throughout Brigit's Isles. The tall stones connect the Earth and the underground Waters to the Air and the Fires of the Sun, Moon and Stars. It is their Goddess Danu who inspired the erection of literally hundreds of stone circles and avenues throughout Britain, including those at Avebury, Boscawen-Un, Tregeseal, Callanish, Stenness, Castlerigg, Ballynoe, Brodgar, Merry Maidens, Nine Ladies of Stanton Moor and Long Meg and Her Sisters. Standing stones are also found in quantity in Brittany in France and in smaller numbers all over the world.

The Goddess visible in the shapes of the hills and valleys by Marian Elliott

The Ancient British Goddess

In late neolithic Britain the Great Mother Goddess of all was An, Ana, named for the beginning of all things from the first sound on the outbreath Aaaaaa....nnnnn....aaaaa. She was Spinner of the Thread of Life, Weaver of the Web of Connection and Cutter of the Thread at Death. She was Goddess of the natural elements and all the directions. She was visible in the shapes of hills and valleys, clothed by the many colours of Her Nature.

Her healing vibration could be felt beside the springs which flowed out from Her body. The clear, clean streams splashing over Her earthy flesh gave health to human populations. Bodies of water and rivers were important in the neolithic and for hundreds of years, as sources of food and as a safe way to travel, where the land was thickly wooded and might be a hiding place for wolves, savage boars and other dangerous creatures. Since the rivers flowed from Her Body their sources were also openings into Her Underworld Womb. They were named after Goddesses.

Brigit gave Her name to the rivers Brue, Brid and Brent in England, Braint in Wales and Brigit in Ireland. Danu gave Her name to the Danube in Europe. The Irish River Boyne was named after the ancient Cow Mother Bo, Boand, who like Hathor in the Egyptian pantheon was the Giver and Sustainer of Life through the nourishing milky waters which flowed from Her udders/breasts.

The Shannon and the Liffey took their names from the Goddesses Sinnann and Life. (*The Serpent and the Goddess* - Mary Condren.) Wells and springs were named for Bride, Ana and Madron

A sacred spring in Cornwall emerges from the depths of the Mother's body

and other local Goddesses whose names were later taken over by Christian saints.

The land too was called after the Goddess. Eire takes its name from the triple Irish Goddesses Eriu, Banbha and Fodhla. In one of the Keltic tales the invading Sons of Mil meet the Triple Goddess. They are told by Her that if they wish to enter Ireland and be fruitful and prosper, they must honour the Goddess. So they called the land Eire after Eriu. Scotland was named after the Winter Hag Scota. And the Isles of Britain? Some say the name comes from the Isles of Prydein, but in these days of the Goddess's return we know these are truly Brigit's Isles.

The annual cycle of the seasons of the Goddess with colder winters and warm summers was and still is marked by eight Sunfire festivals and thirteen monthly cycles of the Moon. These cycles were encoded in the positions of neolithic standing stones within and aligned to stone circles, and in the orientation of ritual mounds and passage graves towards the rising and setting sun or moon on particular days of the year. For example, Brugh na Boinne or New Grange in Ireland, is aligned to the rising sun at the Midwinter Solstice. The Clava Cairns in Scotland were aligned to the Winter Solstice sunset.

Passages to some ritual mounds are aligned to equinox sunrises. Stones in the inner circle at Avebury are aligned to Beltane and other

Opposite: In the magical St Necten's Glen near Tintagel in Cornwall, water springs forth through a Yonic opening in the rocky body of the Goddess.

Author standing in one of the three great mounds of the Clava Cairns near Inverness in Scotland

sunrises. Sites such as Callanish are aligned to the rising or setting of groups of stars, such as the Pleiades or Orion, at particular times of the year. Built 4-6,000years ago these alignments are no longer true because the solar system has moved onwards in its own travels relative to the background stars, but science is able to calculate their original orientation.

The Cycle of the Goddess's Seasons

The Goddess was very obviously present in Brigit's Isles in the past in neolithic, bronze age and later Romano-Keltic times. Today She is returning to our consciousness and one of the primary ways in which we can experience Her is by honouring Her through the cycle of the seasons of Her Nature and the turning of the Sacred Wheel of the Year.

Many indigenous and pagan cultures use Ceremonial Wheels to honour the energies which influence and direct the life of the people. In ceremony priest/esses, shamans, medicine teachers and healers work with the powers of the Sacred Wheel to help maintain a harmonious relationship between the people and the earth we live upon, between the physical and the spiritual spaces which we inhabit. In Brigit's Isles there are eight sunfire festivals on the Sacred Wheel of the Year. These are natural spiritual festivals in that they mark specific times in the astronomical relationship between the Earth and the Sun, which are expressed through the changing of the seasons of the year.

The Wheel of the Year in Brigit's Isles

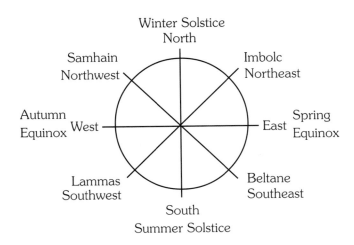

The Sacred Wheel of Brigit Ana/Britannia

I first described the Sacred Wheel of Ana the Great One in *Spinning the Wheel of Ana* (Ariadne Publications 1994). The teachings of that Wheel explore the nature of the Goddess Ana as She expresses Herself through the cycle of Her seasons. As the wheel turns with the year different qualities of the ancient and present day Goddess are revealed through eight sunfire festivals of the year.

As with all wheels the Sacred Wheel of Ana turns and understanding of its meanings are refined with each revolution. In this new edition of *The Ancient British Goddess* I introduce changes to Ana's Wheel which have emerged through its use in ceremony and sacred drama over several years.

The primary change is that I now name the Wheel of Ana as the Wheel of Brigit Ana, Brit Annis, She who is Britannia. I want to reclaim Britannia out of the martial role given to Her in historical times, honouring Her as primary Goddess of this land. It is appropriate to include Brit within Her name since Brigit is one of the most well loved and remembered Goddesses of these isles.

Each of the eight directions on Britannia's Wheel has associated Goddesses, qualities, elements, colours, power animals and some Gods and we shall explore all these. We shall look in greater depth at the mythology and landscapes of the Goddesses who are connected to the four crossquarter fire festivals of Imbolc, Beltane, Lammas and Samhain, which are times of the year when the Goddess was traditionally honoured in the past and is being celebrated again today. These festivals lie half way between the solstices (winter and summer - the shortest and longest days of the year) and the equinoxes (equal hours of night and daylight). Imbolc lies halfway between the winter solstice and spring equinox; Beltane lies halfway between spring equinox and summer solstice; Lammas is half way between summer solstice and autumn equinox; and Samhain is between autumn equinox and winter solstice.

Astrologically the crossquarter festivals occur at 15 degrees of the appropriate Sun sign on the ecliptic, i.e. at 15^0 Aquarius for Imbolc, 15^0 Taurus for Beltane, 15^0 Leo for Lammas and 15^0 Scorpio for Samhain. In the present day however the festivals are more usually celebrated at the turning of the calendar months, e.g., Beltane is now marked around May 1st, when it could more accurately be celebrated around May 5th or 6th. Another way to mark these special times is

Ancient British Goddess

Britannia – Lady of Brigit's Isles

Foosiya Miller

through the Lunar festivals in which a ritual space is opened for two weeks from the new to full moon in the appropriate sun sign connected to the festival.

On Britannia's Wheel the four elements of Air, Fire, Water and Earth are assigned to the four cardinal directions of north, east, south and west in a new and original way. Air is placed in the North, Fire is in the East, Water is in the South, and Earth is in the West. The crossquarter directions express combinations of elemental energies - air and fire at Imbolc, fire and water at Beltane, water and earth at Lammas and earth and air at Samhain. This Wheel is different to the conventional Wiccan Ceremonial Wheel, being a ninety degree revolution onwards from that Pagan wheel.

The reasoning for this is given in detail in *Spinning the Wheel of Ana* and briefly as follows, beginning in the northeast at Imbolc which is the festival of Brigit the Fire Maiden. In origin Brigit is *breo-saigit*, the flaming arrow that flies through the air. She is a combination of fire and air. Fire is also associated with Rhiannon, whose festival takes place at Beltane in the southeast. She is Goddess of the fire of passion, sexuality and love. As a mediator between the worlds Rhiannon carries a torch to light Her way. I therefore placed Fire in the east between Brigit and Rhiannon. This means that Air, Brigit's other element, is placed in the north, also connected to the dry withered Cailleach of Winter and the airy mountains of inspiration where birds of prey live.

As White Mare from the Sea Rhiannon is born from water, so Water is placed in the south, which leaves the Earth element in the west, the direction of the setting sun's nightly descent into the earth. Earth is connected to the Underworld (under Ground), Samhain Sow of the northwest and to the abundant and fruitful Lammas Mother Goddess in the southwest.

Another change to the Wheel of Ana comes in the attribution of colours to the eight directions. When I wrote the earlier book, influenced in part by other traditions, I thought it correct to place the four Old European Goddess colours of red, white, black and yellow in the four cardinal directions. I have now returned to my original understanding which was demonstrated in the 1992 sacred drama *Spinning the Wheel of Ana*. I have assigned these Goddess colours to the four crossquarter directions when the Goddess is traditionally honoured. White is in the northeast at Imbolc, Red in the southeast at Beltane, Yellow in the southwest at Lammas and Black in the northwest at Samhain. Each quarter of the wheel, e.g. north to east, east to south, etc., can be

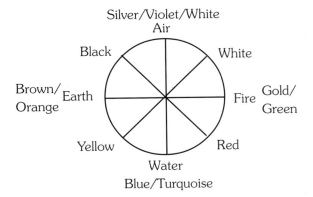

viewed as having one of these four colours or one of four additional colours given to the four cardinal directions . These are now associated with the colours of nature - Green/Gold in the east for springtime and sunfire, Blue/Turquoise in the south for water, Brown/Orange in the west for autumn and the earth, and Silver/Violet/White in the north for winter snows.

Distinctive Goddesses of the English, Welsh, Irish and Scottish pantheons are associated with each of the eight directions., but basically the four Elemental Mother Goddesses are associated with the four cardinal directions and the fourfold Goddess as Maiden, Lover, Mother and Crone is assigned to the four crossquarter directions.

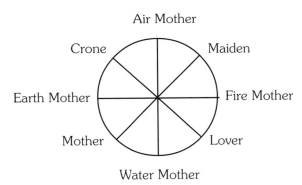

For the Elemental Goddesses of the North, East, South and West, I have chosen those Mother Goddesses who were honoured by our earliest known ancestors, who lived in the lands of Wales, Ireland, Scotland and England. Drawing them forth from our own forgetting we are once again celebrating these Goddesses in the present day in our ceremonies and songs. We are bringing them back into life through our prayers, worship, study and creative expression. The gifts of these Goddesses

Ancient British Goddess
The Sacred Wheel of Brigit Ana/Britannia

North /Winter Solstice
AIR/VIOLET-SILVER
Wren/Eagle/Owl/Buzzard
Sceptre/Sword/Feather Fan
Mother of Air
Danu, Anu, Arianrhod
Bone Woman, Stone Woman
Cailleach, Tyronoe

BLACK/Samhain/Northwest
Crone Goddess
Dark Mother, Keridwen
Sheela na Gig, Mazoe
Crow/Sow/Toad
Cauldron/Sickle/Scissors

Northeast/Imbolc/WHITE
Maiden Goddess
Brigit, Bridie,
Kernababy, Thitis
Swan/Snake/Cow/Wolf
Grael/Spindle/Spinning Wheel

West/Autumn Equinox
EARTH/BROWN-ORANGE
Mother of Earth
Banbha, Brigantia
Gaia, Moronoe
Boar/Badger/Fox
Stone/Orb/Crystal

East/Spring Equinox
FIRE/GREEN-GOLD
Mother of Fire
Artha, Grainne,
Eostra, Cliton
Bear/Hare/Hen/Cat
Wand/Rod

YELLOW/Southwest/Lammas
Mother Goddess
Ker, Grain Goddess,
Madron, Glitonea
Deer/Stag/Horned creatures
Loom/Shuttle

Southeast/Beltane/RED
Lover/Virgin Goddess
(Ke)Rhiannon, Olwen, Elen,
Blodeuwedd, Thetis
Mare/Horse/Dove/Swan
Comb/Mirror/Shell

Mother of Water
Domnu, Queen of the Deep
Lady of the Springs and Wells
Lady of the Lake, Gliten
Chalice/Shell
Dolphin/Whale/Salmon/Seal
WATER/BLUE/TURQUOISE
South/Summer Solstice

Opposite: The Totem Creatures of Britannia's Wheel drawn by Willow Roe

have remained constant through time to the present day. In the following sections I will describe these Elemental Mothers keeping in mind all that has gone before in this introduction.

As we explore the mythology of our native Goddesses we will also look at the sacred sites which were built for their worship in the past. I have selected Goddesses for Britannia's Wheel who embody characteristic elements from English, Irish, Welsh and Scottish mythologies. We will focus on particular aspects which are related to the time of year for each Goddess, yet we will keep in mind that each Goddess contains all the others too. Like a hologram a small fragment can lead us to the whole. She is One and Indivisible. When relevant I will also give details of Her God consort.

Mythologically each crossquarter Goddess can appear with three or four aspects. She is the Maiden, the Lover or Virgin, the Mother and the Crone, transforming at will from one into the other. However following the cycle of Her Nature, one aspect of the Goddess tends to predominate at any particular season of the year - the Maiden Goddess at Imbolc, the Goddess as Lover and Virgin at Beltane, the Mother Goddess at Lammas and the Crone or Dark Goddess at Samhain. We shall concentrate on these individual aspects in order to demonstrate the annual cycle of worship of the Goddess through the turning of the seasons in Brigit's Isles from spring to summer to autumn and winter.

In a change from Ana's Wheel I have moved two Goddesses into new positions on Britannia's wheel which through experience seem to be more appropriate to their attributes. The whole wheel is a Sun Wheel encompassing the movement of the earth in relation to the sun throughout the year but in order to understand the qualities of the Sun Goddess Grainne on Ana's Wheel She was located in the southwest. On Britannia's Wheel, Grainne moves to the East to share the role of Fire Mother and Goddess of Springtime with Artha the She Bear and Eostra. In addition I have placed Brigantia in the west as Lady of the Land.

On the Wheel shown on the previous page I have included the names of the Nine Morgens who rule the Isle of Avalon as given by Geoffrey of Monmouth. They are nine sisters, three triple Goddesses and nine aspects of the one Goddess. Eight of the Morgens circle the wheel with the most famous, Morgen la Fey, the Lady of Avalon at the centre.

I have found through experience that Britannia's Wheel is a wonderful tool for invoking the presence of the Goddesses of this land. I currently use the Wheel as a foundation teaching for a year long training for Goddess-loving people to Self-initiate as Priestesses and Priests of Avalon. It is the wheel upon which the Glastonbury Goddess Temple, the first modern day public Goddess Temple in Europe for a thousand years, is being founded.

In the following sections of the book we will explore Britannia's Wheel as a means of describing and understanding the multifaceted expressions of our native British Goddesses. We begin at Imbolc with the Maiden Goddess Brigit.

Brigit the Maiden

Brigit, Bridie, Bringer of Light
Kele-Keeper of the original sight
Nineteen Maidens tend your hearth
Goddess of healing and smithcraft

Bride of the White Hills   (chorus)
Bride of the Golden Hair
Bride of the Sun and Moon
Mary of the Gael

Blessed poetry spoken by the well
Brigit of healing with a magical spell
She is the White Swan, wings outspread
Flying southwest, dreaming ahead

Serpent Bridie, hidden in the earth
Cow Mother Brigit giving of your wealth
Wolf Clan Woman teach us what we need
The touch of your wand quickening the seeds

Dakini Woman, illuminate our Sight
Rattle your drum that rolls in the night
Snowdrop Queen, sacred Milk Maid
Give to us your fecundating flame

Brigit's Holy Well by Marian Elliott

Brigit is the Goddess revered from the earliest times throughout Britain and Europe. Originally She was the universal Goddess - the Maiden, Lover, Mother and Crone who reigned over all the elements of earth, water, fire and air. Over time She has become particularly associated with the Maiden aspect of the Goddess, with fire and the

Opposite: Goddess Brigit by Foosiya Miller

39

Maiden Brigit

Spark of Life within all living things. She is particularly honoured at Imbolc, the first of the four crossquarter festivals of the year, celebrated at the beginning of February. Brigit presides over fire, air, springs and wells, healing, purification, poetry, inspiration, transformation, all the arts and crafts, youth and immortality. The colour of Her direction is sparkling Maiden White.

It has been suggested by Mary Condren in *The Serpent and the Goddess*, that the name *Brigit* originally meant *Goddess* and was the name for all Irish and British Goddesses. So to call the British Isles *Brigit's Isles* is be true to our origin as Goddess-loving peoples. The Irish form means *high* or *exalted*. The name *Brigit* comes from *breo-saigit* meaning *fiery arrow*. She is a *Dakini* or *sky dancer*. Born of the Great Mother, She is the bestower of divine gifts and mystical knowledge.

Brigit the Triple Fire Goddess

Brigit is the triple Fire Goddess. She is Bride, Brigit and Brighde (Bridie), symbolising three different kinds of fire. She is the fire of inspiration, the Muse - the Goddess of poetry spoken beside the sacred well. The word poetry comes from *poesis*, meaning creation. To speak poetry is to sing the world alive. In ancient times poets were the keepers of the ancestral memories who sang or spoke poetry and lived under Bride's blessing. Ollaves of the Druid order in Ireland carried a silver or golden branch with tinkling bells in Bride's honour marking Her passage.

Brigit's fiery Sacred Hearth, by Marian Elliott

Brigit is Goddess of the Hearth-fire, the fire that is in the home and in the smithy. From the earliest times the hearth has been at the heart of every home - the source of light, heat and warm food. A new house is not a home until Brigit's flame has been lit upon its hearth. This flame is taken from the hearth of MaMa, the maternal grandmother, so that the flame of Bride is a perpetual flame that goes on burning through the generations. Today with central heating and no chimneys in our homes our Goddess altar becomes our hearth, where the candle flames of our love for Her can still burn.

Stone marking the site of St Bride's Healing Well now covered over, beside the River Brue (also named after Brigit), in Glastonbury

Brigit is the Goddess of Healing at the sacred well. There are many St Bride or St Bridget's Wells all over Brigit's Isles where Her healing waters still flow. At these lovely wells we can drink and immerse ourselves in Her healing waters which are rich in minerals and Her fiery efficacious vibrations. Here we can tie ribbons and pieces of material to nearby thorn bushes, so that they flutter in the wind like prayer flags, taking our prayers and hopes for healing to the Goddess's ear. As the cloth is torn to rags by wind, sun and rain, illnesses and griefs too fall away. Many of these wells which are dedicated to St Bridget were originally dedicated to the earlier Goddess Brigit.

Brighde is also Goddess of Smithcraft, the fiery alchemical art of melting metals and creating beauty. In the ancient world the blacksmith and the shamanka or shaman were equally honoured as having access to the Otherworld. The shamanka entered the magical land of the Goddess via ecstatic trances in which she communed with Brighde. The smith knew the magic which created the shining copper mirrors and costume decorations in which the souls of the dead could be caught and helped into the Otherworld or where missing fragments of the soul could be glimpsed and so retrieved.

Brighde is Lady Alchymia, She who heats us up in Her fiery vibration, melting the base metal of our personalities into the gold of our souls, all impurities into Wisdom. She is equated with Sophia, the Greek Goddess of Wisdom, who is sought by alchemists in their quest to find the Philosopher's Stone (the Stone of Sophia) and the Elixir of Life. Brighde opens the gateways for us to contact the Fires of Life.

Maiden Brigit

Early British Shamanka and Shaman with the tools of their craft

Marian Elliott

As the Fire Goddess of Poetry, Healing and Smithcraft, Brigit is the inspiration for the healer and shaman/ka who seeks to know the ways of fire, who is able to contact and communicate with the ancestral energies and who can heal the sick in mind and body. I experience Brigit as a really ancient and universal Goddess, who brings with Her a healing and transformative vibration, especially beside fires, sacred wells and springs.

Names of Brigit

In mythology Brigit is identified with Danu, Anu or Ana or later was said to be Her daughter. She is also equated with the Goddess Kele, Kale, Cale or Kali of the Indo-European Kelts. A Kele-De was mistranslated in medieval times as Bride of God, when it means Spirit of the Goddess Kele, but the allegiance to Bride can be seen. Kildare in Ireland was an early shrine of the Goddess Kele or Brigit. Her priestesses were known as *kelle*. Irish writings described Mary Magdalene as being a kelle or sacred harlot, one who offered the experience of the Goddess through her sexuality. Kelle was Christianised as the mythical St Kilda who ruled the western paradise of the dead.

In the Western Isles of Scotland Brigit is named as Bride of the Fair Palms and Mary of the Gael. In stories, hymns and poems recorded in the *Ortho Nan Gaidheal* at the end of the 19th century by Carmichael, Brigit is often equated with the Virgin Mary. She is also said to be her midwife and a wetnurse to Jesus. She was called the Godmother of the Son of God and Christ is said to be the Foster Son of Bride. In the Hebrides Bride was the Divine Midwife who cared for all mothers and their babies.

Brigit's Sacred Animals

Brigit has four sacred animals - the Snake, the Cow, the Swan and the Wolf, four aspects of Her nature. Snakes were kept in Brigit's shrines where Her oracles were given out through communion with the chthonic energies of Bride the Serpent Creatrix. Brigit is the nurturing Sacred Cow who like many creatures of the White Goddess is white with red ears. Like the Egyptian Hathor Her plentiful milk feeds Her human children. She is the White Swan who flies between the watery emotional realm and the mystical heavens and in Her fourth aspect She is the Wolf, one of the totem guardians of Brigit's Isles.

Brigit the Snake

Brigit was worshipped in Scotland as the regenerative Serpent, which lived in the ground beneath Her oracular shrines. The emergence of the snake from its hibernatory hole in the earth at Imbolc was regarded as an auspicious sign for the coming year.

Statue of St Brigid with emblems of cow, oakleaves, snowdrops and sacred flame at Cullin near Mullingar, West Meath, Eire

Maiden Brigit

The regenerative Snake reemerges from beneath the oracular Omphalos stone at Imbolc, by Marian Elliott

Opposite page: Brigit with Her Totem Animals. Painting by Foosiya Miller

Early on Bride's morn
The Serpent (the Queen) shall come from the hole
I will not molest the Serpent
The Serpent will not molest me

(from *Ortho Nan Gaidheal* by Carmichael, SAP)

The Snake connects the chthonic Underworld energies to the Middleworld where human beings live. As Brigit the Snake symbolises creativity, shapeshifting and transformation.

Brigit, Cow Mother & Milkmaid

Isis the Egyptian Cow Mother

Brigit is the white horned Cow Mother revered throughout the ancient world as the Giver and Sustainer of Life. The Sacred Cow is a symbol for the Great Mother in many ancient and modern cultures. In India She is Kali-ma allowed to roam the streets in freedom even today. In Egypt She is known as Hathor the sacred cow often depicted as a woman with a cow's head, the milk of whose breasts or udders produced the Milky Way in the heavens and who daily gives birth to the sun. As Isis She is a Goddess with a woman's head with cow's horns. For the Native Americans She is White Buffalo Calf Woman, who originated from the Pleiades, the cluster of stars on the shoulder of the constellation of Taurus the Cow/Bull, which they know as the White Buffalo.

As recognition of the Goddess's power waned throughout Europe, the once all powerful Cow Mother Brigit became the human Saint Bridget who lived in Ireland and travelled to England. She is depicted on St Michael's church tower on top of Glastonbury Tor and in carvings in Glastonbury Abbey as a woman milking a cow. In Ireland at Kildare the wide plains of the Curragh were given to St Bridget as pasture for Her

Diana Griffiths

45

Maiden Brigit

St Bridget milking her cow on St Michael's tower on Glastonbury Tor

cows when originally all the land had belonged to Her. Brigit became the Milkmaid and Shepherdess who looks after Her animal and human flocks.

Brigit the White Swan

Brigit the Swan Maiden by Marian Elliott

Brigit is known as the White Swan and is the First Ancestor of the Swan Clan. There are many legends from Britain and all over Europe and Asia of Swan Maidens and Princes who are changed through love, from swans into human beings and back again. Many of these tales involve Swans flying in to land on lakes where they remove their feathers and become beautiful young women. As they bathe they are espied by local young men who fall madly in love with the Maidens and soon wish to marry them. The stories often involve the men hiding these swan feather dresses and the Maidens marrying and becoming *Brides*. After many years and when children have been born the Swan costumes are rediscovered. The Maidens don their feathers once again and fly away only occasionally returning to see their offspring.

Sometimes the stories are of seven brothers said to be enchanted or cursed by a Witch or Old Woman (the Goddess as Crone) They are transformed into Swan Princes who can only be returned to their human form by a young Maiden

who must overcome great adversities to save them. These tales always present such transformations as punishments rather than opportunities to journey into the Otherworldly realms in the forms of swans. These stories are the reversal of earlier traditions in which apprentice shaman/kas earned the right through completing arduous trials to don Brigit's Swan feathers and so be able to fly beyond the earth to the heavenly realms. Once again today in visions and journeys we can travel on the back of Brigit's Swan from watery to the heavenly realms.

Divine Swans date from the earliest times all over the world. Carvings in mammoth ivory of Swan Women with the long necks of swans and women's bodies were amongst the earliest Goddess finds at Ma'alta near Lake Baikal in Siberia. Dating from the paleolithic era they were accompanied by sixteen Goddess figures and the Ma'alta plaque with its seven circuit spirals. (*Lady of the Beasts* by Buffie Johnson)

The Sacred Swan has come down to us through many religious traditions in the form of the Angels who are imaged as having human or light bodies and Swan's wings. Brigit is the prototype for all the Angels. She is the original Lady with Swan's wings. When we invoke the presence of Brigit during a healing session She often arrives in the form of a woman with wings in which She enfolds the person in need of healing. This is a glorious experience.

The Swan Clan gathers at the Swannery at Abbotsbury in southern England to mate and give birth to their young in safety

Beautiful Swan shows her snake-like neck and bird's body

As the White Swan Brigit is the ancient Bird and Snake Goddess in one form, with the body of a bird and a snakelike neck. She is a form of the Plumed Serpent, who was known to the Native Americans as Quetzalcoatl. The Bird and Snake Clans are two of the original Thirteen

The outline of a Swan in flight is formed by the contours of the hills which make up the Isle of Avalon in Somerset

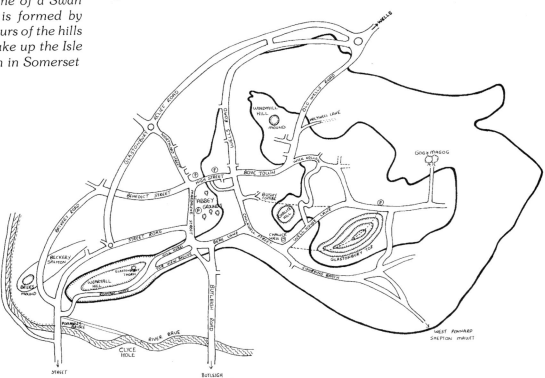

David Dunger

In Avalon in the contours of the sacred landscape an Old Woman can be seen riding on the back of the Swan. She is the Crone aspect of the Goddess in Glastonbury where Brigit is the Maiden.

Maiden Brigit

Snake and Bird Goddess from a model in a shrine, in Thessaly, 5000BCE, by Diana Griffiths

Clans who are said by the Native American Hopi to have emerged out of the earth after the Flood into the present Fourth World.

Marija Gimbutas in the *Language of the Goddess* gives many examples of early Snake and Bird Goddesses from Europe. There are illustrations of carvings, figurines and artifacts from earliest paleolithic through to neolithic times, indicating a widespread and powerful spiritual culture, which honoured both the Snake and the Bird Goddess. Often the Snake and Bird were united in one form as in the Swan or Goose.

The outline of a Swan in flight can be seen marked out by the contours of the hills which make up the Isle of Avalon, at Glastonbury in Somerset, as it rises out of the surrounding Summerland meadows. Here the Swan flies from the northeast, the direction of Brigit on the Sacred British Wheel. In the native American tradition this is also the direction of the Plumed Serpent where the Design of Energy can be found.

In Avalon the Swan flies with her neck outstretched towards the southwest, which for the Native Americans is the home of the Kachinas, who are Star Beings who influence the weather and are called the Keepers of the Sacred Dream. It is they who keep the dream of our world alive. By following the way of Brigit the White Swan, we too may enter the Dream and reach for the stars from which we all come.

Bride of Love

Bride is the original Goddess whom all human Bridegrooms honour when they marry human Brides. All over the world today in another sign of Brigit's return Brides dress in fine, lacy, white Swan dresses, which have ballooning skirts which fluff up like Swan feathers. They veil themselves like the Goddess Bride Herself hiding their beauty from human eyes, revealing themselves to their Chosen One. Like Rhiannon, the Welsh Goddess of Love, Bride too has Her human Bride Groom who takes care of Her needs. At Abbotsbury in Dorset the large flocks of swans which come there to mate, nest and feed are tended by a Swan Herd or Groom.

However as the Maiden Goddess, Bride is actually rarely seen with a consort. The most likely partner to the Dakini Brigit is the Daka, or Archangel Michael, who like Bride has Swan's wings and is also associated with fire and high places. Like other Dakinis Bride is often depicted carrying a white rod, the symbol of Her secret consort.

Brigit the Wolf

The Wolf is one of the Guardian creatures of Brigit's Isles. In the past roamed freely in the forests and woods only finally being hunted out in the last two hundred years. The Wolf represents a darker face of the normally radiant healing Goddess. Images of St Bridget often show Her in the company of a wolf or dog, who protects Her from harm. A stained glass window in St John's Church in Glastonbury is one such depiction. Another can be seen in St Bridget's church at Kildare in Ireland. Brigit's festival of Imbolc continued in Roman times in the festival of Lupercalia, from *lupus* meaning wolf. Celebrated on February 15th Lupercalia was dedicated to Romulus and Remus, the twins who were reared by a Wolf Mother and who later founded the city of Rome. Interestingly as Brigit emerges into our awareness once again wolves are being reintroduced into some of the wilder places of Scotland.

Goddess of the Sun and Moon

Bride is the Sun Goddess who gives life to all that lives on the Earth. Without the Sun there would be no life. In ancient times the Sun was regarded as feminine in many cultures, including the Gaelic, and the

The Sun Goddess sets over the top of Chalice Hill in Avalon

Maiden Brigit

Opposite above: Bride's Well at Imbolc on the Hebrides. Painting by Monica Sjoo 1989
Below: Avalon at Imbolc - the lake turned to ice.

Moon was seen as masculine. In some cultures both Sun and Moon were regarded as feminine - twin sisters. It is in patriarchal cultures that the Sun is thought of as male and the Source of Life and the Moon is female, though of course it is connected to women's menstrual cycles. Bride is known in Ireland as Bride of the Golden Hair shining as the Sun and Bride of the White Hills and the Moon. She is honoured on the tops of hills and greeted in the rising and setting sun and moon.

Brigit's Number Nineteen

Brigit 's energy encompasses the relationship between the Sun, the Moon and the Earth and is particularly connected to the number Nineteen. In each solar year of twelve months there are thirteen moons which usually overlap into the following year. It takes 18.67 (19) years for the Sun and Moon to move through their cycles of major and minor standstills and return to an original place of relationship to one another. The number 19 marks this relationship.

Nineteen Maidens, Faerie Queens or Crones are said to tend Brigit's sacred Fire Light, which burns continually in Her Shrines. At Kildare 19 nuns tended St Bridget's Fire and on the 20th day it was said that Brigit Herself tended the flame. Like the Native American Tsalagi, Brigit's Maidens knew the secrets of Fire and Her shrines were lit with the Rainbow Light which emanated from their own bodies. Initiation into Brigit's Mysteries takes 18.67 years.

The nineteen stones of the Merry Maidens in Cornwall

Neolithic peoples understood the significance of the number nineteen (18.67) and many neolithic stone circles are made up of nineteen standing stones. Several of these are found in Cornwall, such as the Merry Maidens, Boskawen-Un, Tregeseal and Boskednan stone circles.

The Callanish Stones on the Hebridean Isle of Lewis were specially positioned so that every 18.67 years the full moon can be seen from the stones rising so close to due south that its path across the sky is less than 2 degrees above the horizon. The moon appears and disappears, gleaming through notches in the mountains revealing the body of the Sleeping Beauty. (*New Light on the Stones of Callanish* by Margaret and Gerald Ponting).

Boskawen-Un in Cornwall is a ring of 18 granite stones plus a nineteenth made of white quartz in the west. In the centre is a leaning phallic pillar.

Colour opposite above: Lanyon Quoit in Cornwall
Below: Sone head near Avebury decorated with flowers by June Peel

Britannia on a £10 note

Britannia

Britannia or Brigit Anna is a combination of Bride and the great Goddess Anna. She is a goddess of the grain whose picture still appears on British bank notes. Over the centuries She has been given a more martial role, being used by politicians to support war. Cartoonists gave Her a helmet like Greek Athena, a spear and a shield, although She still holds a sheaf of grain in Her lap. The shield was originally Her sun disc symbol of Her role as Sun Goddess. Her spear represents again Her secret consort. The elements of the earlier bountiful life-giving Mother Goddess are there for those with eyes to see in the most established of icons.

Maiden Brigit

Brigantia the Land of Brigit

The Latin form of Brigit's name, Brigantia, is found throughout Britain and Europe. As well as being the name of a Goddess, (see Mother of Earth) later Brigantia was also the ancient realm which included neolithic Britain, Brittany and northern Spain. Brigit was worshipped in Roman times in Britain and Gaul but undoubtedly was a much earlier Goddess.

According to Robert Graves She is connected to the Aegean Goddess Brizo, *brizein* meaning to *enchant,* to whom votive ships were offered. Many neolithic ritual mounds are built near to the sea, some in the form of large ships with ritual spaces and burial chambers in the centre. One such is a huge remarkable tiered mound at Barnenez in Northern Brittany, built on a hill by the sea near to Morlaix. The stony outline has a bow and stern and the whole mound looks like a large ocean liner.

A Romano-British sculpture of Brigantia by Diana Griffiths

Brigit in India in the form of one of the Sapta Matrikas, the Seven Divine Mothers, She too carries a white rod of regeneration. Rajasthan 6th century CE.

Diana Griffiths

54

Imbolc, Festival of the Maiden Bridie

Bridie's feast day comes at the beginning of February at the crossquarter fire festival of Imbolc or Oimelc, which lies halfway between the Winter Solstice and the Spring Equinox and celebrates the Maiden Goddess. Imbolc means *lustration, ewe's milk* or *purification*. It is the time when the first lambs of the year are born and the first milk of the ewe signals the burgeoning of new life in the depths of winter. Bridie is said to *breathe life into the mouth of dead winter*. In these days the first rays of Bridie's Sunfire light begin once more to illuminate the dark days of winter. Imbolc is not the beginning of Spring, but a reminder that Spring will come in a few weeks time at Spring Equinox. At Imbolc Bridie receives the rod of power from the icy hand of the Cailleach, the Old Crone who has held it since Samhain (end of October) through the winter. As She takes the rod in Her hand once again the green cloak of Her nature begins to spread across the land and Bridie's flower, the snowdrop, begins to bloom. Images of Brigit as Brigantia show Her carrying Her white rod of power.

Snowdrops blossom in their thousands at Imbolc in Snowdrop Valley on Exmoor

Maiden Brigit

With the touch of Her rod Bridie quickens the life lying dormant in the seeds in the earth, in the roots of plants and trees, so that they begin to stir, readying themselves for the uprise of the energies of spring-time. Bridie is the Quickener whose light touch stirs the life force within us, quickening the ideas and dreams which lie dormant within our souls.

Several neolithic sacred sites are aligned to sunrise or sunset at Imbolc, including the Castlerigg stone circle in Cumbria which is oriented towards Imbolc sunrise.

The Star of Bride, Brigit's Cross or Bride's Eyes

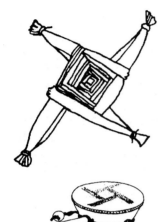

At Imbolc the Star of the Bride also known as Brigit's Cross, and Bride's Eyes are made out of the dried reeds or the stems of corn or barley and twisted into the shape of a swastika. The swastika is a very ancient symbol which in its clockwise form represents the rotation of the Earth. This symbol is also sacred to both the early Native Americans and the Tibetans and is found on the double-sided Kachina rattles in both cultures. The swastika was abused by Nazi Germany for evil purposes but of itself is a neutral energetic symbol showing the movements of the four elements and four directions.

Bridie Dolls

It was traditional in Brigit's Isles to make Bridie Dolls at Imbolc and examples were recorded by Carmichael at the turn of the 20th century. In Scotland the older women of the family would shape a sheaf of dried barley into the likeness of Bride and decorate Her with sparkling jewels, early snowdrops and primroses. The Star of the Bride was pinned next to Her heart. On Imbolc Eve the Bridie Doll was brought to the door of the house and the women called out to those inside,

"Let Bride come in! Let Bride come in!"

The women of the house would reply,

"Bride! Bride! Come in, thy bed is made.
Preserve the house for the Triple Goddess
(A.Carmichael)

Top: Brigit's Cross made from reeds or corn or barley stems at Imbolc
Above: Tibetan rattles depicting Brigit's Cross also known as the swastika

The Bridie Doll was placed next to the fire in a cradle with a straight white wand of birch, broom or white willow which represented Brigit's secret consort and Her transforming rod of power. The fire in the hearth was allowed to die out and the women levelled the ashes. In the early morning on Bride's Day the ashes were scanned to see if Bride's wand had left its mark in the dust. There was great joy if such marks were found as it meant Bridie had come and blessed the house for the coming year.

Over the last 15 years or so we have renewed such customs of making Bridie Dolls at Imbolc in Glastonbury. Traditionally these dolls are made out of straw or grasses, which are burned and returned to the earth at Samhain. As we have been reawakening Goddess consciousness in ourselves and our community we have made our dolls out of more substantial materials, sewing into their bodies our hopes and dreams for the coming year. New Bridie Dolls are welcomed into the circle of Mother and Grandmother Dolls who are accumulating Goddess wisdom for the whole community.

Ewe's milk and small honey and barley cakes are served as part of the Imbolc festival. Dried ears of grain from the previous year's harvest are planted in the ground ready to sprout and become the new year's harvest.

Four Bridie dolls from Avalon held by four Glastonbury women - Thalia Brown, Oshia Drury, Lydia Lite and Diana Griffiths.

Brigit's Talismans

Brigit has three principal talismans - the Spindle or Spinning Wheel, the Bell and the Grael of the Maiden. As the Maiden Goddess Brigit is Spinner of the Threads of Life and Fate. Her first talisman is the Spindle or Spinning Wheel whose continuously spinning form created the first long threads of animal hair and plant fibres that were sewn and then woven into cloth, marking a major step forward in human development. In other traditions She is known as Spider Woman or Grand Mother Spider who spins the Threads of Life and Fate and who created the first human beings on earth. Like the Native American Pipe of Peace the Spindle is both a sacred symbol and a practical object. It contains both female and male elements with its central Yonic opening within a circular disc into which is fitted a long Phallic shaft. To spin is to continually recreate the harmony and balance of the universe.

St Katherine's church overlooks the Swannery at Abbotsbury in Dorset with stunning views over the sea

The introduction of the Spinning Wheel allowed more thread to be spun more quickly, so that the arts of sewing and weaving developed. As the Gift of the Fire Goddess this Wheel is imaged as the fiery spinning Katherine Wheel and Katherine the Most Pure is equated with Brigit. At Abbotsbury in Dorset St. Katherine's Church stands on a high conical hill overlooking the Swannery, where thousands of Bridie's swans come to feed through the winter months and to give birth to their babies in safety in the spring.

The Spindle and Spinning Wheel are the first elements in the fourfold cycle of Brigit Ana the Weaver. The others are Rhiannon's Comb which cards plant and animal fibres, the Mother's Loom and Shuttle on which the Cloth of Life is woven and the Crone's Scythe or Scissors which cuts the Thread of Life at death.

Brigit's second talisman is Her tinkling Bell carried by those who speak Her words of inspiration. The sound of Her Bell opens the gateways to the Otherworld, calling the Barge to Avalon.

Brigit's third talisman is the magical Grael of the Innocence of the Maiden Goddess, that space of openness, complete trust, fearlessness and virtue. In Arthurian legend this is the shimmering mystical Holy Grail which was sought by the heroes of the Round Table, the Holy Grael which was always held in the hands of women. On the Grael Quest those who enter the Castle of the Grael must ask the right question,

"Whom does the Grael serve?"

And know the answer, before the Grael of the Maiden becomes their own.

Wayland's or Brigit's Smithy

Wayland's Smithy is a long barrow dating from 2850 BCE, sited on the crest of a rolling hill next to the Ridgeway and near to the Uffington White Horse/Dragon in Oxfordshire. In the neolithic era long barrows were dedicated to the Goddess as Mother of the Dead, with their long stiff bodies and vulval entranceways and womb-like interiors. Their remains are found all over Brigit's Isles every 20 miles or so, built in different styles but all having similar functions. They are places where the bones of the dead were buried, where ceremonies and feasting took place in their forecourts, and the tribal ancestors were contacted.

At Wayland's Smithy a womb-like burial chamber lies at the eastern end of the barrow and is entered through a narrow vaginal passageway. The long body of the barrow is made of white chalk, which in its original form was a mound 5 or 6 metres high and 55 metres long. It must have gleamed on the crest of the hill from afar in the moonlight and shone in the sunshine, marking the home of the Mother of Death and Regeneration. Although its origins and purpose are much older, Wayland's Smithy is named after the much later Norse Smith God, Volund. It might more appropriately be called Brigit's Smithy, dedicated to Brigit as Goddess of Smithcraft and Maiden of Rebirth.

The vulval entrance into the womb/tomb of Wayland's Smithy long barrow which might more appropriately be dedicated to Brigit

In *The Wayland Saga* translated by K M Buck, Wayland and his brothers espy three Maidens sitting by the water having removed their Swan feathers for a spell. The brothers fall in love with the Swan Maidens, whose names are all Bride. They court and soon marry the three fairy Brides. One day after years of happy marriage, the Brides find their Swan feathers once again and putting them on they turn back into Swans and fly away to the west.

The Isles of Bride

Opposite: Stone circle of Callanish on Lewis, one of Bride's Isles

Bride gave Her name to several islands off the coast of Britain. The Hebrides in northwest Scotland comes from *tHe-bride's - the Bride's*. The ancient Long Island of the Outer Hebrides, which when sea levels were lower included the Islands of Uist, Barra, Harris and Lewis, was called *Eileana Bride - the Isle of Bride*. The magnificent neolithic standing stones of Callanish (Cal's or Kale's headland) are to be found here.

Bride, Iona and the Fountain of Youth

As the Maiden Bride is the Goddess of Youth and the Immortality of the Ever Young. In legend Bride is said to have lived as a child on the

small Scottish island of Iona. High on this beautiful island is a hill called Dun-I or Slibh Meanach. On top of the hill there is a magical spring known as the Fountain of Youth. To drink this water is to taste the immortality of the Maiden Bride.

Above: the author beside the Fountain of Youth on top of Dun-I on Iona, a holy island off western Scotland

Maiden Brigit

There is a prophecy retold by the famed mystic Fiona Macleod who was the writer William Sharp, in her book *Iona,* which foretells that,

"......the Divine Spirit shall come again embodied through mortal birth in a Woman, as once through mortal birth in a Man. She will be a new Presence and Power. She will appear white and radiant in the hallowed gardens of the soul and where we wander on Her hills the Shepherdess shall call us home."

Iona is a superb place of wind, wildness and peace in which to feel Bride's immortal presence.

The Sanctuary at Avebury Sacred to the Imbolc Maiden

The Sanctuary lies to the southeast of Avebury and the concrete posts which can be seen today mark the remains of an ancient circular timber hut and a stone circle. The first wooden temple on the site was 65ft in diameter and dates from 2,700BCE at the same time that the inner mound of Silbury Hill, which has the same diameter, was also built. Michael Dames in *The Avebury Cycle* suggests that where Silbury Hill is the Lammas Mother in the sacred landscape, the Sanctuary represents the Imbolc Maiden.

In 2,600BCE the wooden temple was replaced with a stone circle 130ft across at the same time that Silbury Hill was built to a height of 130ft. West Kennet Avenue was also constructed at this time connecting the Sanctuary to the central Avebury Henge. Michael suggests that the Sanctuary was the Temple for Puberty Rites for young women and is sacred to the Maiden Goddess.

Bride on the Isle of Avalon

The Isle of Avalon with its naturally formed Swan-shaped body was obviously dedicated to Brigit in the past. According to legend there was a shrine to Goddess Bride near to Glastonbury at Bride's Mound. This truth was later christianised when St Bridget was said to have come to Glastonbury and lived on Bride's Mound at Beckery or little Ireland in a hermitage dedicated to Mary Magdalene, the kelle.

St Bridget's Chapel was later built on Bride's Mound and her embroidery tools were preserved there. The nuns who lived on the Mound were said to celebrate Easter at the Aries full moon and to live in tune with the cycles of the Moon. The chapel has now disappeared, but the Mound remains although today the town sewage works cover part of its slopes (!). A lovely stone marks a now sealed Bride's Well. Bride's Mound is one of the gateways to the mysterious Isle of Avalon. The Friends of Bride's Mound are at present attempting to save and restore this ancient sacred site from the hands of unsympathetic developers.

Brigit's bag of healing herbs and Her bell are said to be hidden in the ground near to Chalice Well in Glastonbury. Occasionally the bell can be heard ringing in the meadows behind the well.

The low rise of Bride's Mound at Glastonbury surrounded by flood waters

St Bridget of Kildare

St Bridget of Kildare is clearly linked with the earlier Nature Goddess Brigit. Images of St Bridget show flames coming from Her head just as they did from that of the Sun Goddess. She too is connected to milk, red-eared cows, fire, sun, serpents, wolves, healing and smithcraft.

Goddess pilgrims with Brid and the children and the author(first from the left) and Sister Mary Minehan of Solas Bride (3rd from the right) at Kildare

Historically St Bridget is associated with the foundation of a convent of nuns and a monastery for monks at Kildare in Ireland. Her main symbol was the sacred oak tree from which Kildare is said to take its name - Cill Dara - Church of the Oak. Kildare is near to Dun Ailinne, another ancient holy site where the Goddess Ailinn had Her sacred fire.

There are many stories of the Perpetual Fire which burned in the monastery at Kildare. There are memories of an earlier time when Brigit's flame burned in Her holy shrine. This fire was tended by nineteen Maidens, kelle or nuns, who guarded the flame in a twenty day cycle, one for each Maiden. On the twentieth day Brigit Herself was said to

The site of St Bridget's Fire Temple, now a square but once it was round

tend the flame. The Sacred Fire was concealed behind a circular hedge of shrubs or thorns and no man was allowed to enter. Those who dared went mad or burst into flames and died. The place of the original fire shrine is marked by a small square enclosure beside the church on top of the hill at Kildare which must originally have been round.

There are records of a famous college at Kildare, whose head was regarded as an incarnation of the Goddess and who was called Brigit when elected. It is very likely that the monastery and college were founded on a holy site, which had been sacred for centuries to the ancient Goddess Brigit. St Bridget is said to have drawn the boundaries for her monastery by spreading her cloak over the ground, just like the Goddess Brigit, as far as it would reach. It was a very large green cloak, the cloak of Nature. St. Bridget was given the vast meadows of the Curragh to graze her cattle.

The lovely St Bride's Well at Kildare beside the Curragh. Note Brigit's Cross on the arch.

Maiden Brigit

In recent years the Perpetual Flame which once burned at Cill Dara in Bridie's honour has been relit by Brigidine nuns, who run a centre in Kildare called *Solas Bride*. They are happy for Goddess and Christian pilgrims to visit them and will guide visitors to Brigit's local sites and to St Bride's Well.

St Brigit's Wells are found all over Ireland and in England, some like that at Cullin near Mullingar, have been beautifully restored and honoured in the present.

Beautifully restored Brigid Well at Cullin near Mullingar, Eire

Brigit's Brehon Laws

According to Mary Condren, Brigit was the original Lawmaker of early Ireland. She is the force behind the Brehon Laws first recorded by Christian monks in the seventh and eighth centuries CE. They had been memorised for generations before by both women and men *brehons*. These laws were particularly favourable to women even after they had been purified by St Patrick and the Christian monks and continued for many centuries.

They provided for the satisfaction of women's intimate sexual needs in marriage and extensively covered the rights of women in marriage, divorce and in pregnancy out of wedlock.

The Perpetual Flame

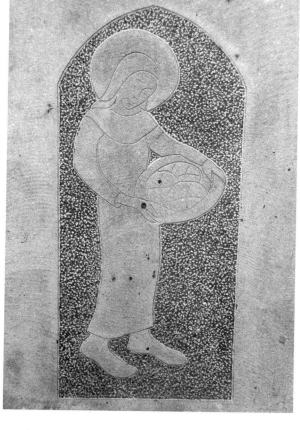

Some say that Bride's Fire Shrines similar to the one at Kildare are to be found elsewhere in Brigit's Isles, wherever fires burn at high places and including one at Bride's Mound beside the Isle of Avalon. Here Her perpetual flame still glows in the hearts and minds of those who love Bridie on Her magical Swan island.

Altar carving of St Brigid with Bridie Cross buns at St Brigid's Well, Cullin near Mullingar, Eire

Brigit's Sacred Flame by Marian Elliott

Mother of Fire
Artha, Grainne, Eostre

Mother of Fire

Pattern of the stars of the Great She Bear

Bear Mother holding her cub fom Yugoslavia c.4500BCE drawn from "Language of the Goddess"by Marija Gimbutas

The Mother of Fire in the East at Spring Equinox is Artha the Great She Bear, Grainne the Sun Goddess and Eostre, Goddess of Springtime.

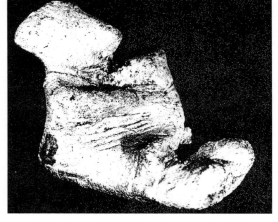

Artha is Ursa Major, the Great She Bear in the heavens, the pattern of stars also known as the Plough. Artha is the Mother of the Fire that is in all the stars and in the centre of the earth. She is Fire on the hearth in our homes and in our hearts. She is the Bear Mother who traditionally gave birth to human beings. In Sanskrit Her name means *abundance, riches*. She is the Fire that brings light, warmth and life to all the world. She is the waxing Moon drawing the waters of the earth towards Her.

Artha was connected in European mythology to the Earth Goddess Ertha or Eortha and to Art, Artio, Ars, Ursel, Ercel and Artemis Calliste, who was also called the Great She Bear. King Arthur, the British hero/ king, whose name comes from the Welsh *Arth Vawr* or *heavenly bear*, is Goddess Artha's sacred son, spouse and consort.

I have suggested earlier that the Irish Race of P(artha)lon may have worshipped Artha the Bear Mother. They were the people who built the great chambered long barrows and mounds still found all over the western fringes of Brigit's Isles. When these mounds were being built Artha's bear offspring still roamed the forests. Hunted by early humans their bodies provided food and warm furs for palaeolithic and neolithic peoples. Passages in neolithic ritual graves are aligned to special sunrises and sunsets, when fingers of light penetrate dark womb chambers sometimes illuminating carvings. They are wonderful places in which to contact Artha the Great She Bear and Grainne the Sun Goddess, also a Mother of Star and SunFire

Above: entrance to Hetty Pegler's Tump, a neolithic chambered long barrow north of Uley in Gloucestershire, which is oriented to the equinox sunrise.
Right: Beautiful ammonite at the entrance to Stoney Littleton chambered long barrow near Wellow in Somerset

Mother of Fire

Grainne, Sun Woman

In Scots and Irish Gaelic, Greine or Grian is a feminine word meaning the Sun. Dia Greine is the Sun Goddess, or Sun Mother who in English I shall call Grainne. From all the indications in the earliest languages of Brigit's Isles the Sun was a feminine being, known to be the Mother of All Life on earth. In the daytime She shone Her golden light and warmth onto the world. At sunset She descended beneath the sea or into the waters of the earth through wells, ponds and lakes o regenerate the world. In the summertime She blessed the earth with Her fiery energy and brought all plants and grain to fruition.

Grainne and Diarmuid

Giant's Grave - a gallery grave, also known locally as the bed of Dermot and Graney near the enchanted Lough Gur in Munster, Eire

In the Irish Romance of Grainne, Greine or Grania and Diarmuid, Grainne the Sun Goddess compels Her lover, who is Diarmuid the Moon God, to follow Her, while Her husband pursues them for a year and a day. The lovers travelled around Ireland spending each night in a different dolmen. Many of these passage graves are known as the beds of Diarmuid

and Grania. The story describes the cycle of the solar and lunar year. It is one form of the early myth found in many other parts of the world in which the Moon God is compelled through love to follow his Solar Mistress around the world, appearing and disappearing as his vigour is replenished and exhausted in making love.

Trethevy Quoit in Cornwall is another bed of the Goddess and Her lover. The capstone has a prominent hole in it through which light may have shone into the original darkened womb chamber.

Mother of Fire

Dolmens are groups of three or more standing stones with a large capstone on top. Built in the neolithic age as burial mounds and ritual sites they were originally covered in earth or small stones appearing as large mounds from the outside. Over the millennia the earth and stones have blown away revealing the stone skeleton at the core. Burial mounds have different designs in different parts of Briigit's Isles. They are known as passage or gallery graves or dolmens and in Cornwall as quoits.

It is interesting to note that the sound of the Gaelic name for the Sun Goddess, Greine or Grainne, is the same as the English *grain*, the generic term for the seeds of cereal crops, whose cultivation revolutionised human existence on Earth at the beginning of the neolithic era.

The Lion Mother

Sun Goddess flanked by twin lions on an early seal from Krete.

In Europe the Sun Goddess was Cybele, the Mother Goddess who carries a solar disc in Her hand, which later became a tambourine, drum or shield. Cybele is often flanked by two lionesses. An earlier form of the Sun Mother was found at Çatal Huyuk in Anatolia, in which the seated figure of the Goddess is flanked by two lionesses or panther-like creatures as a baby is born from between Her legs. This Birthgiving Lion Mother dates from 6,000 BCE and was found in a grain bin.

Britannia, Goddess of Brigit's Isles sits with a round shield which was originally Her Sun disc, by Her side and She is sometimes pictured with Her Lion. The Lion is found on many British coats of arms.

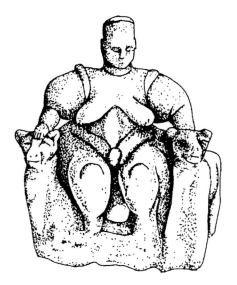

Figurine of the Birth-giving Mother with Lions at her side from Çatal Huyuk, dating from 6,000BCE

Diana Griffiths

72

As wild cats were domesticated the Lady of Lions became the Cat Goddess worshipped throughout Europe.

Sulis

In Roman Keltic times the Sun Mother Goddess in Brigit's Isles was known as Sul or Sulis, whose warm healing waters flowed up from beneath the earth at Bath. Large baths were built in Her honour. As the Sun sank beneath the waves at night Sul warmed the waters of the world, which emerged at sacred places as Her healing waters. Her role was later supplanted by the Sun God Apollo and Sul was subsumed to Minerva, the Roman Goddess of healing, crafts and war, a difficult trinity to combine.

Grianan

In Scotland high sunny places were known as *grianan*, the abode of the Sun. In Ireland a grianan is a round sun room or sun terrace where women sat, played and worked together and from which men were excluded. It was the place where Women's Mysteries were explored. It was also the name given to large earth works situated on the top of hills or in lakes. The magnificently restored Grianan of Aileach in County Donegal in Ireland dating from 1700 BCE is dedicated to Greine, the feminine Sun; to Coill, a masculine Moon; and to Ceachta, the stars. (Janet MacCrickard, *Eclipse of the Sun*). A *grianchlochit* was a Sun-stone, a crystal used to focus the Sun Goddess's rays to make a special Sunfire.

Neolithic Sun-Sites

Many British and Irish neolithic sacred sites were dedicated to the Sun Goddess as the Giver and Re-newer of Life. Their entrances are oriented so that on the Winter Solstice or at the Equinoxes the rising and setting sun's rays penetrate to an inner Womb/Tomb space. The great mounds of Brugh na Boinne and Knowth in the Boyne valley in Ireland are two magnificent examples. Stones lining the inner passageways of both of these sacred mounds are decorated with many symbols of the Sun Goddess - multiple circles, sun rays and eyes.

Eostre, Ostara

The Fire Mother in the East is also Eostre or Ostara, a form of Astarte, who is also a Queen of the Stars. Hers is the energy of the Spring Equinox when light and darkness are held in equal measure. She brings all of Nature alive igniting the Fires of Life in the seeds lying beneath the ground, in the roots deep in the earth. In Her season sap rises in plants and trees and animals, birds and human beings respond to Her call to become sexually active. The bright green of Her Springtime

Eostre's pale yellow primroses blossom at Spring Equinox

nature appears in plants and trees. The colour of Her direction is Green/ Gold and Her talisman is the Magic Wand or Rod of Fire of the Mind who represents the Priestess's Secret Consort and fertilising Force.

The Christian festival of Easter comes on the first Sunday after Eostre's Aries Full Moon. Eostre's Red Hen's eggs are exchanged as symbols of rebirth after the dark days of winter. In the past particularly in eastern Europe, the eggs were usually coloured red, the colour of life and menstrual blood.

Eostre's companion creatures are the Bear, the Moon Hare, the Red Hen and the Cat. The Moon Hare became the Easter Bunny who is magically able to lay eggs. Witches are said to be able to assume the form of hares or cats and according to Barbara Walker in her wonderful *Women's Encyclopedia of Myths and Secrets*, Queen Boudicca's banners bore an image of the Moon Hare.

Cats of all kinds have long been associated with the Goddess from Cybele with Her lions to the Egyptian Lion-headed Sekhmet and the Cat Goddess Bast, to Britannia with Her lion, to Scandinavian Mother Freya who rode in a chariot drawn by cats. As well as being the Great She Bear Artemis Calliste (Artha) was called the Mother of Cats and was identified by the Greeks with Bast.

At the Spring Equinox we celebrate Eostre, Artha and Grainne honouring the fires of the heavens and in the earth. The gifts they offer us are warmth, enthusiasm, the fire of the mind, passion, creativity, protection, strength and courage.

"Wild Eve", a Cat Woman sculpted by Foosiya Miller.

Rhiannon the Lover

Welcome to my Orchard, Lord Pwyll of the Summerland
Now you have drunk from my chalice,
Behold in joy my true form.

Chorus: For I am Rhiannon, the Triple Goddess
        Revealed in every woman's womb,
        I wax to fullness, wane and die
        Each cycle of the silvery moon

I once was Queen in the Summerland
No king could rule without me
I am the White Mare that rides from the sea
No fleshy horse with whom druid lore
Entreats you the king to spend his seed.
    Chorus
From Annwn to Earth I shall return
With you I shall walk upon the bones of giants
Make love in the Orchards of the Western Isles
But first before we may lie together
You must conquer foes, yourself among them.
    Chorus
You who have taken the horns of Kernunnos
You who changed places with Arawn
You who has drunk from Mab's blood chalice
Eat this my gift of the apple of wisdom
And place this (apple) in the mouth of him who is reborn.
    Chorus
I am your beloved, awake in your dreaming
Call for my help when danger is near
Beware of a bird whose colours are hidden
Battle where white and red waters blend
Slay the tyrant with a single bow
    Chorus
      (From THE SHINING ONES by Kathy & Mike Jones)

Opposite: Rhiannon of
the Birds, White Mare
from the Sea by
Foosiya Miller

Rhiannon the Lover

There are several Goddesses in British mythology who particularly express the qualities of the Goddess as Lover at the Beltane Fire. They are the Welsh Rhiannon of the Birds, Olwen of the White Track, Elen of the Trackways and Blodeuwedd the Flower Goddess. In this section we shall focus primarily on Rhiannon with Olwen, Elen and Blodeuwedd at the end.

Rhiannon the White Mare

Rhiannon is the Goddess as Lover, the Lady of the Beltane Fires and the Goddess of Love in Brigit's Isles. She is the ancient White Mare from the Sea who rides between the lower, middle and upper worlds. Sacred since the earliest times She was worshipped here long before horse Gods were introduced to Britain by the Saxons. She is also known as Rigantona the Great Queen, and as Epona the White Mare. In Europe She was known as Mare-headed Demeter in Mycaenae and as Leukippe the White Mare in matriarchal Krete.

There are many figurines of Her as the Keltic Epona of Gaul in which She always appears with Her horses. She either sits astride or side saddle on a horse or is seated between two ponies or foals. In this bronze figure from Wiltshire Epona sits between two foals and has a yoke against Her left shoulder indicating Her connection to the introduction of agriculture in the late neolithic. Like the Grain Goddess She has ears of corn in Her lap.

Epona seated between two foals with a yoke over her shoulder.

Rhiannon, Goddess of Love and Sexuality

Rhiannon is the British Goddess of Love. She is the Goddess of Springtime blossoms and the sexual awakening and flowering of Nature. As She opens Herself to life so the sap rises in the plants and trees, and animals and human beings become sexually active. She carries a flowering branch of hawthorn or apple blossom. Her colour is red, the red of life blood, menstruation, fertility and sexuality.

Like Aphrodite She is born from the white waves of the sea and is often imaged with a comb in one hand and in the other a mirror or a shell held to Her ear, listening to the sounds of the sea, the ocean of emotion. She is the sexual Goddess seen riding her horse in the nursery rhyme at Banbury Cross.

> "Ride a cock horse to Banbury Cross
> To see a fine Lady ride on a white horse.
> With birds at her shoulder and bells on her toes.
> She shall have music wherever she goes."

Her Cockhorse consort is still represented in May Day folk festivals in the country towns of Britain, such as the annual Beltane gathering at Padstow in Cornwall, in which ritually masked men ride hobby horses and chase women. The Cockhorse is also visible in the phallic Maypole which is plunged into the fertile Earth on May Day and around which couples dance and interweave coloured ribbons.

In folklore the stories that surround Rhiannon are those of love between the Goddess and human beings. Underlying these stories is an ancient initiation into the Mysteries of the Goddess through love, through falling in love with and surrendering to the Goddess in the form of a beloved woman. Like a wild white mare, Rhiannon is powerful, instinctual and untameable. She responds only to love. She must be approached directly with the honour and respect due to Her.

Rhiannon as the Beltane Goddess bringing blossoms.

Thalia Brown

Rhiannon's white horses ride to shore on the crests of the waves

The White Mare from the Sea

Rhiannon is imaged as a White Mare rising from the sea. She is the White Horse that dances on the crests of the waves, as they ride to the shoreline. She is the Goddess of the land Her waves touch. Her horse's feet measure the land which belongs to Her. She appears as a beautiful woman riding a white mare and surrounded by clouds of birds. Her robe is red, blue, green or gold, edged with white swan's down and Her hair is the colour of red/gold honey. Her eyes hold such mystery that those who look into them will ever hope.

The Queen of Faerie

Rhiannon is associated with the *sidhe*, the magical mounds and hollows hills of legend. She is Queen of Faerie and rides Her white mare between the lower, middle and upper worlds. She is Queen of the Cross Roads, that intersection between the inner and outer landscapes. She is equivalent to the Kretan Goddess Rhea, Mistress of Time, and encounters

Opposite: Rhiannon, Queen of Faerie by Thalia Brown

with Her happen out of time. A day in Her world is often a year and a day in the ordinary world. Those who journey into Faerie land often don't return for tens or hundreds of years.

Rhiannon appears as the Queen of Elfland (the home of the *Elfs* or *Aelfs*, from the Saxon English meaning *Shining Ones*) in the Scottish tale of the poet Thomas the Rhymer. Thomas of Erceldoune was a 13th century poet who lived near the Eildon Hills in the Scottish borders. One day he was lying on Huntlie Bank when the beautiful red-haired Queen of Elfland or Elphame dressed all in green, came riding by on Her milk-white horse. Its mane was hung with silvery bells which tinkled as she moved.

Their eyes met and Goddess and poet fell instantly in love. Climbing up behind Her on the mare Thomas was taken by the Queen to a garden where She fed him on bread and wine and lulled him to sleep in Her lap. The Queen made him renounce Christianity and initiated him into her World under the name of True Thomas. Thomas stayed in Elfland for seven years and during all that time did not speak, for he knew that if his mortal's voice was heard in Elfland he would never return to his own country.

After seven years Rhiannon decided that it was time Thomas returned to the Middleworld. She gave him an apple which when eaten would ensure that he could never tell a lie. At first he didn't want to eat it, but on the Queen's insistence he took a bite. On his return to his own country his family and friends were delighted to see him, having long given him up for dead. He wrote a long poem about his time in Elfland which made him famous as a poet and he became known as Thomas the Rhymer. He found that once he had eaten the apple he could not lie, and he was able to foretell the future. He became famous as a prophet.

A few centuries later in 1597 in the Scottish witch trials Andro Man confessed to carnal knowledge of the Queen of Elphame.

"She is very pleasant and will be old and young when she pleases. She makes any King whom she pleases and lies with any she pleases."

Like the serpent in the Garden of Eden, Rhiannon tempts us to take a bite from Her apple of wisdom. This apple grows on the tree of the Knowledge of Good and Evil and allows us to learn discrimination between truth and lies. It is the fruit of love between humans and the divine. Rhiannon enjoins us to surrender to love, to cease lying and to receive Her inspiration.

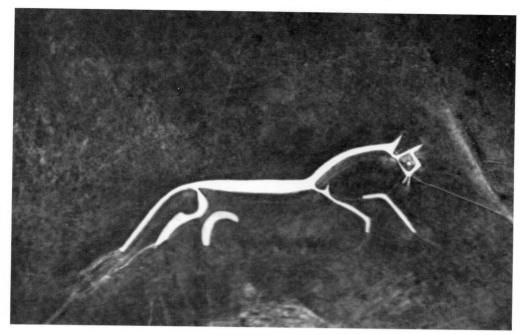

Ashmolean Museum

First Ancestor of the Horse Clan

The White Horse or Dragon of Uffington can only be see in its entirety from the air.

As the Great White Mare, Rhiannon is a primal Ancestor of the Horse Clan. On the Sacred British Wheel the Mare lies in the southeast. According to Native American tradition the southeast is the home of the Ancestors and is directly connected to the Pleiades. One of the ancient names for the Pleiades is the Seven Daughters of Aphrodite or as they would be called in British mythology the Seven Daughters of Rhiannon.

One of the most potent images of the Horse Clan can still be seen in the outline of the Uffington White Horse, carved in the chalk overlooking the Vale of Pewsey in Oxfordshire. It is believed to have originally been shaped like a Dragon and there is an ancient connection between horses and dragons. It is currently dated to the second millennium BCE. One really interesting feature of this Horse/Dragon is that like the huge Nazca landscape outlines in Peru, its whole shape can only be seen from above by beings in the sky. Of course at the time it was constructed there were no aeroplanes. Who is to say that our Mare Ancestors were not the Seven Daughters of Rhiannon who came to Earth from the Pleiades? They may have arrived in fire-breathing vehicles that looked like dragons, bringing with them the knowledge that tamed the wild horses.

Rhiannon the Lover

Following pages:
Opposite: Painting of Blodeuwedd by Jane Brideson
Next page: The Lake of Llyn y Fan Fach from which the Lady of the Lake emerged
Following page: Rhiannon of the Birds by Thalia Brown

The later sacrifice of horses to Saxon Horse Gods was a corruption of the earlier honour shown to the Great White Mare. Their bloody rites and strange sexual perversions in which kings were supposed to have sex with mares(!), veiled an earlier shamanic initiation into the powers of the Horse Clan.

In many native cultures, such as those in Siberia and North America, a Horse gives the shaman/ka the power to travel between the Lower, Middle and Upper worlds. The horse carries the traveller through the gateway to the Lands of Death and Immortality, journeying to retrieve lost parts of the self. Today the psychic journeyer, shamanka and healer ride the White Mare between the worlds, into the hollow hills and the worlds of Faerie.

Rhiannon of the Birds – the Muse

Surrounded by small birds, Rhiannon is the Muse who gives inspiration to poets and artists. The Sirens who appear in the Welsh Triads and the Romance of Branwen singing with wonderful sweetness are called Birds of Rhiannon. There are usually seven or nine of them, variously described as small birds - tits, warblers and chaffinches; as white birds, such as doves or swans; or as blackbirds or ravens. The Seven Sisters of the Pleiades were known also as the Seven Doves.

This beautiful statue of the Queen of Heaven's Dove descending is in the cloisters of Iona Abbey.

In many cultures doves belong to the Great Goddess and the Queen of Heaven, symbolising peace, purity and sexual passion. Christianity took the peace and purity and discarded the sexuality of the dove, but times change. This lovely statue in the middle of the cloisters of Iona Abbey shows the connection between the descent of the Dove and the Goddess's Yoni.

Rhiannon's birds bring poetry and inspiration. They sing us to sleep or waken the dead in the apple orchards of the Western Isle. They give solace to the lonely and unfortunate. On the night before the Keltic heroes came to kill him, the Giant Yspaddaden Penkawr wished that Rhiannon's birds would come and sing to him, before the Lady on the White Horse took him away to the Land of Souls. Rhiannon leads the dying and those on the path of transformation to the mysterious Western Isle of the Dead, to await healing and rebirth. Legend tells that when King Arthur was dying he was taken to Avalon, the Isle of the Dead, by nine Blackbirds.

blodeuwedd

nine buds of plant & tree, long & white are

nine powers of nine flowers, nine powers in me combined,

my fingers as the ninth wave of the sea

Rider Between the worlds

Rhiannon rides Her White Mare between the worlds. She is Goddess of the Tri-via, the threefold intersection between the Underworld, Middleworld and Upperworld. She guides us through the gateways to the lands of Death and Immortality. She leads the dying soul and those on the path of transformation to the mysterious Western Isle of the Dead, where they may receive healing, regeneration and rebirth.

As She journeys She is accompanied by Her birds and sometimes by a dog. This may be a triple-headed dog, similar to the snarling Cerberus of Greek myth. In other places it is a single dog who stays devotedly at Her side, leading the White Mare between the worlds.

The Night Mare

In Her darker aspect the White Mare becomes the Night Mare who haunts our dreams, arousing the Shadows which frighten us into waking, sweating with fear. In the Dreamtime Her nests are to be found in rocky clefts or in the branches of enormous hollow yew trees, sacred to the Death Goddess. They are built of carefully chosen twigs and lined

Willow Roe

with white horsehair and the feathers of prophetic birds. They are filled with the jaw bones and entrails of poets. (*The White Goddess* by Robert Graves)

Sovereignty, Goddess of the Land

Rhiannon is a Goddess in Wales (Waels or Waelshi is the name of a horse-god) and Lady of the Summerland, an old name for Somerset and also for the sunny Western Isles. She is Sovereignty, the Great Queen Rigantona, Goddess of the land of Britain with whom all British Queens are identified. Kings of Britain must marry Her ritually and symbolically in order to rule in peace and harmony.

In Arthurian legend Queen Guinevere is Sovereignty, whom Arthur must marry in order to rule as King in Brigit's Isles. As Goddess, Guinevere may love whom She chooses, but this was forgotten by later patriarchal story tellers who called Her an adulteress when Her favours were freely given to Lancelot. As in Rhiannon's tale in the Welsh Mabinogion, Guinevere's story is that of the demise of the original triple Welsh Goddess Gwenhwyfar or White Spirit (Phantom).

Our present day monarchy still contains remnants of the Royal relationship between Goddess and monarch. The adoration and fervour of ordinary people for our present Queen and some of her family, is the same as that due to a Goddess and Her offspring. Despite human failings archetypally the Queen expresses certain beneficent qualities of the ancient British Goddess, including a love and care for all of her people.

As the betrayed wife of Prince Charles, the heir to the throne, Princess Diana was the latest in a long line of British Royal women who embodied Rhiannon's qualities as the Goddess of Love and who suffered the same fate of betrayal and castigation by the family into which she had married. Diana's tragic death triggered a huge public outpouring of grief which was out of all proportion to the event itself. In her life Diana expressed many of the acceptable and unacceptable faces of the Feminine in this patriarchal land and her death was experienced by many as the death of a Goddess.

Rhiannon's Talismans

Rhiannon has three main talismans - the Comb, the Mirror and the Shell. The Comb is depicted on many neolithic carvings hanging around the neck of the early Goddess. Combs are often shaped like the Goddess Herself, the teeth forming Her skirt and the handle Her body. The Comb also appears in early paintings and on later Pictish stones, sometimes in the hand of a Mermaid or Horsewoman, who often also holds a round Mirror. Rhiannon combs Her long red-gold hair, which represents the vegetation which covers Her earthly Body. The Comb symbolises the Spirit of the Wind as it blows through Her hair. The Mirror represents the shining Sun which gives us all life.

The Comb combs Her White Mare's coat and is also the carding comb used to card and clean the wool of sheep, goats and other domestic animals. It is used to straighten the wool which is then spun into threads and woven into cloth. It is associated with the important development in the use of animal hair and wool for weaving into cloth for warmth, protection and decoration.

The Mirror, like Alice with her Looking Glass, allows entrance into the Otherworld. It brings the gifts of reflection and of scrying, the foretelling of the future.

As the White Mare from the Sea Rhiannon is born from the waves. Like Aphrodite sometimes She stands in a Shell or holds a Cockle Shell to Her ear as shown in many figurines of Venus/Aphrodite from Europe. The Spiral Shell always symbolises the presence of the Goddess of Life and is found in many neolithic carvings. Held to the ear the sounds of the sea, the place of our primal origins, can be heard.

Carving of a Mermaid with comb and mirror, the Goddess of Love from the sea, in Zennor Church in Cornwall

Beltane – Festival of the Goddess of Love

Rhiannon's festival is Beltane or Belteine, the Maytime Festival celebrated around May 1st. Its name is thought by many to be derived from the Sun God Bel, but Janet MacCrickard has reclaimed this name for the Goddess. She says that *Bel* is not the God Bel, but means simply *bright, white, beneficent* and *goodly*. *Teine* is a feminine form, meaning *solar fire*. Beltane is therefore a festival of the beneficent feminine Sunfire. (*Eclipse of the Sun*, Janet MacCrickard)

Beltane is celebrated at the end of April and the beginning of May, its aura continuing to 15 degrees of Taurus, around May 7th. Mythologically Beltane is a time when the gateways are open between the human world and the mysterious Otherworld. These openings are to be found in the hollow hills, magical mounds, the sylvan forests and

The hollow hill of Glastonbury Tor where Rhiannon rides Her White Mare between the worlds. The terraces visible on the sides of the Tor mark the pathway of a seven circuit Goddess Labrynth.

ancient sacred sites into which the Goddess and the God of the land retreated long long ago, when they were no longer openly honoured and revered by the people. The gateways to the Otherworld are found all over the world from Avalon to Avebury, from the Irish *sidhe* to the hollow mountains of Tibet and the kivas of the Native Americans. They are the places where the veils between the visible and invisible worlds are thinner. Beltane is a time when Rhiannon can be seen here riding Her White Mare between the worlds.

Beltane Eve is the night when Gwyn ap Nudd, (White Son of Nudd or Night), the Lord of Annwn (the Underworld), is said to ride out with the Wild Hunt sweeping the souls of the dead into the Underworld. April 30th is known in Europe as Walpurgisnacht, the night when witches are said to fly up the spiral mountains. My own experience twenty years ago of walking into the three-dimensional spiralling Goddess Labrynth on Glastonbury Tor on Beltane Eve carried such potency.

On Glastonbury Tor there are seven levels of terracing which wind back and forth, up and down the steep slopes, in the pattern of the Kretan Labrynth of the Goddess. This pattern was sacred throughout

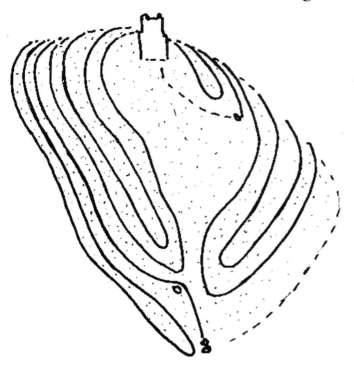

Pathway through the multi-dimensional Goddess Labrynth on the slopes of Glastonbury Tor. This seven circuit Labrynth is found all over the ancient world dedicated to the Goddess.

the ancient world. It is found on early coins from Krete in both round and square forms. It is carved on rocks at Tintagel in Cornwall and it is known to the Hopi Indians as Tapu'at, Mother Earth. Its pattern describes the journeys of the Hopi people through the seven worlds of Creation. At the present time they say that we are moving from the Fourth World into the Fifth World of Peace and Plenty. The design is also found at Pompeii, in Ceylon and Indonesia as well as many other places.

On Beltane Eve twenty odd years ago we began walking the Labrynth as the sun was setting and the full moon rose in a clear and calm sky. By the time we had encircled the Tor back and forth seven times and reached the middle of the Labrynth three hours later, a gale was blowing with thunder and lightening and sheets of rain. We had literally spun up a storm that was physically and psychically transformative. We ran down the Tor, returning a few days later to complete our journey out of the Labrynth. The initiation of the Tor Labrynth Goddess had only just begun.

Beltane is a time for lovers, when trysts are made beside the Sacred Fire to stay together for a year and a day. This was the old way of counting the days of the year when there were thirteen lunar months of

Labrynth carved in a rock face at the wonderful Rocky Valley near Tintagel in Cornwall

Rhiannon the Lover

twenty eight days each, plus one day to complete the solar year. Lovers jump the Beltane Fire together to seal their agreement to journey with the Goddess of Love.

In Scotland at Bealtain all fires were extinguished and the *tein eigin* or need fire was magically produced from the Sun on the Sacred Mound. A large fire was built up and then divided into two and all the people and cattle rushed through between the fires as a blessing and a safeguard for the coming year. People relit their home fires from the communal need fire. This practice survived until the 1920's. (Carmichael)

Mayday

On May day morning the Sun is said to give three joyful leaps in the sky as She rises at dawn. It is a time for love. Nature is alive, vibrant and fertile. Plants, animals and humans are sexually awakened. The Goddess is full of Her plenty and the phallic May Pole is erected, around which we dance, intertwining the ribbons of connection.

Apple blossoms fill the air with their sweet perfume

May Day itself has long been celebrated as the height of springtime and beginning of the longer days of summer. The heady sexual scents of apple and may blossoms fill the air. May blossom takes its name from the month of May, which in turn gets its name from the Greek Goddess Maia, whose name means *grandmother.* Under the name of Cardea She casts spells using may, hawthorn or whitethorn. The Greeks propitiated Cardea before marriage ceremonies with may blossoms and by burning torches of hawthorn wood, because marriage was anathema to the Goddess. Like the Goddess women were free to make love to whomsoever they chose.

The sexual scent of May blossoms fill the air in the month of May

In folklore hawthorn is said to be an unlucky tree which cannot be cut down or brought into the home without bad consequences. Similarly May was considered an unlucky month when the Christian church encouraged purification through sexual abstinence. But we know that wherever prohibition was imposed by a patriarchal church an original and opposing rite of the Goddess can usually be found hidden beneath the later tradition.

Hawthorn and may blossom have an orgiastic use. In mediaeval times the Goddess Flora was celebrated on May morning by riding out to pick flowering blossoms of hawthorn and dancing around the phallic maypole. May blossoms have for many a strong aroma of vaginal sexual fluids and the Turks used the flowering hawthorn as an erotic symbol. May is the month when all nature is sexually aroused and is the time for sexual expression.

Rhiannon the Lover

Beltane at Avebury Henge

In ancient times at Avebury at Beltane the Goddess's fertile conceptual energies would be aroused and celebrated in the great central henge. Built in 2,600BCE originally there were 98 stones in the great circle of Avebury Henge, which is 1,305ft across with a circumference of one mile. A henge is a ritual site in which a high bank encloses a circular ditch with a flat central area. (In a defensive site the ditch is outside of the bank.) At Avebury the bank was 50ft above the bottom of the ditch which was carved out using antler picks and shoulder blades - an incredible feat. Originally the bank and ditch would have been a gleaming white ring of chalk, set against green surroundings. West Kennet Avenue and the now destroyed Beckhampton Avenues enter the circle in the south and the west. In the middle of the great circle there are two smaller circles. The northern inner circle was 350ft across with 27 large stones and the southern inner circle was 340ft across with 29 stones. Most of these stones have disappeared.

In *The Avebury Cycle* Michael Dames proposes that at Beltane women and maidens would have approached the central henge along

Large characterful stones in Avebury's southern inner circle

David Dunger

West Kennet Avenue from the Sanctuary and men would have come via Beckhampton Avenue from Knoll Down. West Kennet Avenue is 50ft wide and approximately one and a half miles in length and was originally made of 100 pairs of stone set at 80ft intervals. Built at the same time as the Sanctuary circle and Avebury Henge, the stones were all present until the 17th century. The main destruction occurred during the 18th century when land was enclosed and people took the stones for buildings. The remaining stones contain wonderful images of people, animals and ancestors. Touch them, feel them.

Terence Meaden has shown experimentally that rays of light from the rising sun on a neolithic Beltane morning would have penetrated a specially positioned vulvic stone in the southern inner ring. The rising sun at other times of the year falls on nearby stones in the circle.

The Goddess of sexual love hidden with the standing stones at many sacred sites.

95

The horse or lion stone from West Kennet Avenue

The village of Avebury in the centre of the henge was built from destroyed standing stones. The remaining stones have definite personalities containing many faces, vulvas, ancestral shapes, animals and spirits. Use your imagination to see into the stones. Touch the stones, feel their texture and warmth.

Re-Working the Mabinogion – Rhiannon's Tale

Rhiannon's mythic story is told in the Four Branches of the Welsh Mabinogion, which is a long Keltic tale of male heroes and their exploits. Within these stories however it is still possible to detect the essence of the great Goddess Rhiannon as well as Her downfall and humiliation. She is the early Goddess of Love who was forced to withdraw into the Underworld, which in Welsh myth is called *Annwn*.

Rhiannon epitomises the ancient Triple Goddess in Brigit's Isles whose power, love and beauty was forgotten. In legend Rhiannon was accused of murdering Her own child, as with so many Goddesses around the world. She was cast out of society and reviled. As a result She retreated into the Underworld realms within the Hollow Hills where She now dwells, emerging only at certain times of the year in certain places. In describing the myths of Rhiannon I take the liberty of retrieving some of their original meaning and the glory due to Her.

We first began to look at the myths of Rhiannon when my partner Mike and I were writing a sacred drama called *The Shining Ones* (written and first produced in Glastonbury at Beltane in 1989). In this drama we reinterpreted the First Branch of the Welsh Mabinogion as a means of connecting with the early British Goddess in Her many forms. All the female characters in the drama were Goddesses. Our aim was to connect with our early British Ancestors, who were called the Shining Ones or the Tuatha de Danann, the people of the Goddess Danu.

Our version of Rhiannon's story was influenced by Evangeline Walton's vivid retelling of the Mabinogion. It begins on Beltane Eve when Lord Pwyll of the Summerland fatefully enters the realm of Annwn while hunting in the forest. Pwyll inadvertently interrupts the Wild Hunt of the Stag God Kernunnos who is being chased by the Lady and Lord of the Wild Hunt. For his interference Pwyll has to agree to exchange places in the Underworld with Arawn, who is the Lunar Lord of Death, in his annual battle with the Lord of the Burning Sun.

In order to enter the Underworld Pwyll must first drink from the blood-red spring waters of Mab the Giantess.

Mab's Song

Drink from my river! Red river of Life
Drink from the blood that flows from my Womb
Deep in my Body the Moon Dew is gathering
Birthplace of children, blood of the moon.

Aruru the sculptor, the Maker of Adamah
Moulder of red earth, fashioner of kin
Ninhursag Goddess, the blessed of the ages
Made us of earth, infused with Her blood.

This is the red mead, the royal ale of Mab
Maker of Kings, the fountain of life
Bathe in my blood flow, the claret of sages
Stain now your body, oh man made of clay

The red iron rich waters of Chalice Well in Glastonbury splash into a basin shaped like a vesica piscis, the Vulva of the Goddess

Opposite: Lord Pwyll of the Summerland interfered in the Wild Hunt of the Stag God Kernunnos pictured here.

Drink of the wise blood,
Drink from the cauldron
Be born again in the land of the Mare
Drink of Rhiannon, the gateway to heaven
Enter the magical land of Annwn.

(From *The Shining Ones* by Kathy and Mike Jones)

Here Mab represents Rhiannon as the menstruating Goddess of the Earth, whose blood flow is visible in iron-rich springs, such as the one which constantly pours from the earth at Chalice Well in Glastonbury. She is the Goddess whose powerful emotion is felt by women during moontime menstruation.

Pwyll drinks from Mab's chalice and crossing over Her red river, finds himself in the apple orchards of the Western Isles, also known as Avalon. Here he falls asleep and dreams of the beautiful Goddess Rhiannon who sits with Her birds amongst the apple blossom. Pwyll is enchanted by Rhiannon's beauty and falls deeply in love with the Goddess of the land.

In the dream Rhiannon speaks to Pwyll about the journey of initiation which lies ahead and warns him of the dangers which will confront him. She gives him two apples. One for himself which is the Apple of Wisdom, the fruit of the Underworld Goddess. The second apple Pwyll must place in the mouth of Gwawl, his future unknown rival for Rhiannon's love.

When he wakes Pwyll successfully fights the Lord of the Burning Sun on behalf of Arawn, and completing this Underworld initiation returns to his own land. The following Beltane having repaid his debt to the Lord and Lady of the Wild Hunt Pwyll goes to a nearby Mound of Arberth in search of Rhiannon. On the sacred Mound it is believed that no man can spend the night alone there. He will either go mad and die, or receive a great vision. There is no way of knowing which it will be, but Pwyll longs to meet the Goddess he has only seen in his dreams.

As he waits on the Mound he once again falls asleep and Rhiannon appears, riding Her white mare, led by an old bent Crone on a black horse. They are accompanied by Dormath, the Gatekeeper Dog who

The Hill of the Witch at Loughcrew in County Meath in Ireland is one of those magical mounds where the Goddess may be encountered at special seasons of the year

guards the Yonic gate or Death's door. Rhiannon rides naked beneath Her fine white veil. The story is full of the sexual symbolism of the Goddess of Love and Springtime. Rhiannon is the archetypal Bride (Brigit in Her springtime aspect) and model for the Spring Maiden, led by the Cailleach or Winter Hag.

In the Mabinogion tale Pwyll tries to catch up with Rhiannon three times as She rides round and round the sacred mound, sending first his men and then himself after Her. No matter how much he shouts Her name and chases Her on his fastest horse She stills stays the same distance ahead of him. It is only when Pwyll says the correct words to this Goddess of the Otherworld, that Rhiannon pauses in Her travels:

"Lady! For the sake of the man you love best, stop for me!"

Rhiannon replies:

"I will gladly stop for you. And it would have been better for your horse if you had asked sooner."

Pwyll had failed to look after his horse in his desire for Rhiannon. In order to contact Rhiannon there are certain things which must be done and said. We can find Her in the sacred places where She is hidden, in the hollow hills and neolithic mounds, but only if we are courageous and approach Her at the correct times of year. When we do see Her we must ask Her directly to stop for us. And we must care for Her animals.

The love story of the Goddess Rhiannon and Her earthly consort Pwyll continues through the First Branch of the Mabinogion. Before he may marry Her Pwyll must prove himself worthy in the ways of the Underworld. In present day psychological terms Pwyll must face his own unconscious Shadow. It is only after many trials and much delay that Pwyll disguised as a beggar tricks his rival Gwawl into climbing into a little bag which can never be filled - the eternal Womb of the Goddess.

Pwyll stifles Gwawl's protestations by placing the second apple Rhiannon had given him in the dream, into Gwawl's mouth. Gwawl too enters the Goddess's womb-path of regeneration, if somewhat unwillingly, and Pwyll truly earns the horns of the Stag God Kernunnos. He is now fit to marry Rhiannon.

The Demise of a Goddess

Together Rhiannon and Pwyll return to the Middleworld, where through his marriage to Rhiannon Pwyll becomes King in the Summerland and the Goddess is honoured once more on the Earth. For three years Rhiannon and Pwyll are happily married until Rhiannon bears a son, Pryderi (menaing *anxiety* or *Golden Hair*). Unfortunately when he is only three days old Pryderi disappears and when blood is found on the sheets Rhiannon is falsely accused of having eaten him. This is the demise of the Goddess in blood and accusations of murder. It is also an echo of Rhiannon in Her Death aspect as the Devourer, the Carrion Bird Woman or Harpy, who is said to eat Her own children.

In his grief Pwyll, who had wanted a son to become King after him, forgets that Rhiannon is Pryderi's mother and would never harm him; forgets that She is the Goddess; forgets their love for each other and doesn't believe in Her innocence. He orders Rhiannon to stand outside his palace beside the horse block for seven years. Like a domesticated mare She must always be ready to carry his guests on Her back. This is the humiliation of a Goddess !

Rhiannon and Her son Pryderi are symbolically represented by a magnificent mare who gave birth each Beltane Eve to a magical foal, which was never seen. As soon as the foal was born it was snatched away by a Harpy, who is the Bird Goddess in Her Death aspect. One year the mare's owner, Tiernon Twrvliant, decided to hide himself in the stable on Beltane Eve to watch what happened. As soon as the foal was born a huge hooked hand reached through the stable window to steal the foal. Tiernon chopped off the hand and the harpy vanished, instead Tiernon found a baby wrapped in rich clothes. He noticed a resemblance to Pwyll and Rhiannon, and returned Pryderi who had not aged at all, to his parents.

Rhiannon the Lover

*Rhiannon the Harpy
by Thalia Brown*

There was much rejoicing in the palace and Rhiannon was released from Her undeserved punishment, but Her power in the Middleworld had been severely damaged. Her son Pryderi or Golden Hair is part divine and part human and he goes on to later rule the Summerland after the death of Pwyll. But the Mabinogion continues the tale of the downward fall of the Great Goddess, with the descendants of Her unsuccessful suitor Gwawl, taking revenge on Pwyll and his offspring. There is war in the land.

Symbolically this story describes the early honour given to Sovereignty, the Goddess of the Land by human beings and the necessity for those who rule to honour and marry Sovereignty. However once they had tasted power Kings and Princes often forgot that they had only gained the right to rule through the love of the Goddess. They thought themselves great enough to rule alone. They forgot how important She is to the wellbeing of the earth and all human endeavours.

All around us today we see the damage which has been done to our planet by those who feel we do not need to honour the Earth, the body of the Goddess. We see Her lungs (the trees) being destroyed, Her oceans, land and air being poisoned. It is vital for our survival that we remember Her and give Her the love and respect which are due to Her. Through our love for Her the White Mare from the Sea will be drawn forth from Her Underworld domain and welcomed back once more into the Middleworld of the British landscape.

Blodeuwedd, Olwen, Elen

Blodeuwedd is the lovely Welsh Flower Goddess also celebrated at Beltane. In the *Romance of Math ap Mathonwy* She was said to have been created from buds and blossoms.

Blodeuwedd's Song

She is formed from nine blossoms
Nine buds of various kinds
From primrose of the mountains
Broom, meadowsweet and cockle
Together intertwined
>*Long and white are Her fingers*
>*As the ninth wave of the sea*
From the bean in its shade bearing
A white spectral army
Of earth, of earthly kind
From blossoms of the nettle
Oak, thorn and bashful chestnut
>*Long and white are Her fingers*
>*As the ninth wave of the sea*
Nine powers of nine flowers
Nine powers in Her combine
Nine buds of plant and tree
>*Long and white are Her fingers*
>*As the ninth wave of the sea*

This is an adaptation of Robert Graves' *Hanes Blodeuwedd* as a song for the sacred drama *The Sacred Marriage* by the author. According to Graves the ninth flower is the hawthorn as Blodeuwedd is another name for Olwen of the White Track, who is the May or Hawthorn Queen, who leaves a trail of white flowering trefoil where She walks. She is also Elen, Protectress of the ancient trackways across the land.

Olwen is the daughter of Yspaddaden Penkawr, Giant Hawthorn or Whitethorn or May Tree. In *The Romance of Kilhwych and Olwen*, Yspaddaden Penkawr puts all sorts of obstacles in the way of Olwen's marriage to Kilhwych, keeping Her in a castle guarded by nine porters and nine watchdogs. He demands a dowry of thirteen treasures all seemingly impossible to secure. But love conquers in the end.

Here the Flower Goddess is controlled first by Her father and then by the husband who wins Her from Her father. But Olwen is the Goddess of Love. She is free and untameable. She is wild nature, the blossoms and the buds. She is the May Queen and the celestial Goddess of the White Track of the Stars in the heavens.

She is also Elen or Helen of the Trackways, the Protectress of all travellers through the once dangerous countryside. She is still remembered in the name Sarn Helen, an ancient drover's road which leads over the high hills and hidden valleys of Wales.

In the *Romance of Math ap Mathonwy* the Flower Goddess Blodeuwedd is conjured up by the magician Gwydion as a partner for the young Llew Llaw Gyffes (the Lion with a Steady Hand), who falls in love with Blodeuwedd the moment he sees Her. Soon they marry and like Rhiannon and Pwyll for a time they live happily together. One day Llew leaves his bride (Bride) alone at home while he goes off to visit Math. While Llew is away Gronw Pebyr comes by Blodeuwedd's castle hunting a stag. When their eyes meet Hunter and Goddess are filled with love. The remainder of the story tells of Blodeuwedd's attempts to kill the magically born Llew by devious means. Llew can only die if he is struck by a spear which has been one year in the making, and he must be not within a house or without, not on horseback or on foot. All this is done by Llew taking a bath in a roofed cauldron by the side of a river, and standing with one foot on a buck's back and the other on the edge of the cauldron. Whoever strikes him with the magical spear in this traditional initiation pose will cause his death.

In the right season Blodeuwedd persuades Llew to show her this strange position and arranges for Gronw to throw the deadly spear. As he is struck Llew transforms into an eagle and screaming, ascends to heaven. After this seeming betrayal by his creation(!) Blodeuwedd, Gwydion goes in search of Llew and finds the eagle on a tree above a pigsty, home of the great Sow of Death, Keridwen. Transformed back into himself. Llew and Gwydion go seeking revenge on Blodeuwedd.

Blodeuwedd like Lilith before Her retreats with Her maidens away from the world going to the mountains. Walking backwards into a river all Blodeuwedd's maidens drown in the river. Only Blodeuwedd survives. Gwydion catches up with Her and instead of killing Her he turns Her into an Owl. This is meant to be a damnation and eternal punishment

Statue of the Flower Maiden Blodeuwedd originally created for Goddess Conference 2000 by Foosiya Miller, decorated for Beltane by friends of the Glastonbury Goddess Temple.

for it is said that the owl is hateful to all birds. The full story can be read in Robert Graves *The White Goddess*.

Once again as in Rhiannon's tale we must sift carefully through the fragments for the memories of the earlier Flower Goddess who is Self-created each springtime. Blodeuwedd is the Goddess of love whom all men may fall in love with or resist. She can choose Her lovers as She wills, unconfined by marriage or castle walls, leading them to the place of initiation. Like Rhiannon She is portrayed as a betrayer and is hounded out of the communal life into the mountains where She displays Her other face, that of the Owl, who also gave her name to Adam's first love, Lilith.

In many cultures the Owl is the Bird of Wisdom, She who sits on Athena's shoulder, whispering Wisdom into our ears. In the Welsh Triads the Eagle of Gwernabwy (Llew Llaw Gyffes) goes in search of a female companion of exalted lineage As he searches he is told that the Owl of Cwmcawlyd (Blodeuwedd) is the oldest of all the creatures and only the ridge of the land is older than She.

At Beltane Blodeuwedd encourages us to love Her in Her flowering beauty and at Samhain She enjoins us to honour Her Owl's Wisdom.

Mother of Water
Domnu, Lady of the Lake

Opposite: "Queen of the Deep" by Foosiya Miller

The Mother of Water in the South is Domnu. She is Ocean Woman, Queen of the Deep, Mother of the Sea Waters which evaporate into the air forming clouds that ride the winds. Sweeping in across the coasts of Brigit's Isles rain pours from the clouds back onto the earth, seeping deep into the land from which it slowly rises as springs, or flows over the land as rivers which return once again to Her great Ocean.

Domnu's festival in Brigit's Isles comes at the Summer Solstice when the Sun climbs to its zenith in the sky, when all of nature is open to life and Her energy pours out to us. In Brigit's Isles we travel South to sit in the sunshine and to bathe in Her Ocean waves. Her colour is Blue,

Domnu the beautiful and awesome Ocean

Queen of the Deep

Joosiya

the everchanging colours of the sky reflected in water, the colour of clean rivers, lakes and oceans.

She is the Full Moon, a silver globe shining in the night-time sky, drawing us towards Her, filling us with lunacy. All of nature swells with energy, flowers blossom in profusion, trees spread their branches and animals give birth and feed their young from Her bounty. Her companions live in Her waters - Whale, Seal, Dolphin and Salmon of Wisdom and all the creatures that live in the sea.

Domnu is Goddess of the Ocean of Emotion. She can be moist, soft, warm and receptive or cold, dangerous and overwhelming. We swim in Her waters with care and respect. Her talisman are the Sea Shell and the Chalice of emotional wisdom. She encourages us to express ourselves, to be who we truly are. She calls us to mystical surrender within the Oceans of Her nature.

Lady of the Holy Springs and Wells

The Goddess in the South is also Lady of the Holy Springs and Wells which abound throughout Brigit's Isles. Places where water springs naturally from the earth have long been regarded as sacred to the Goddess, the openings into the earth being seen as openings into Her Goddess Body, most often Her Vagina. The waters which flow out of the earth are believed to have different magical healing properties. The water may be good for drinking, clean and pure, and/or filled with minerals. The water may be red with iron representing the Goddess's menstrual blood flow as in the waters of the Blood Spring at Chalice Well in Glastonbury, or smell sulphurous, obviously coming up from the deep Underworld or they may be warm and healing, like the waters of Sulis at Bath.

From the neolithic age onwards stone wells, wellhouses and pools were constructed around sacred springs to honour the Lady of the Waters and to ensure that the water flowed cleanly and could be collected easily for drinking. They were also places for immersing the whole body in the healing water. These wells were tended by holy women and men, healers and poets. In Christian times they became known as Saints, because of the magical healings that often took place at these springs. To this day

Mother of Water

*Opposite: Chalice
Well where the red
waters of Her Blood
Spring emerge from
deep within the earth.*

many wells are dedicated to particular saints when once they were all dedicated to the Goddess.

It was traditional to hang pieces of cloth - clouties, belonging to the sick beside holy wells. These were torn from the person's clothing and hung on surrounding trees with prayers for healing. The cloths fluttered in the wind taking the prayers for healing to the Goddess. As

*Prayer ribbons, clothes
or clouties hanging
beside Madron's well
in Cornwall.*

they lost their colour and fell apart in the wind and rain so the prayers were answered by the Lady of the Well.

12 years ago when we visited Madron's Well in Cornwall the clouties hanging on the trees around Her Well were old and grey, the Well forgotten. Today things have changed. Now the branches of the trees overhanging the healing stream are decorated with new pieces of cloth. Bright prayer ribbons flutter in the wind, carrying messages of hope for healing from Her Holy Waters. Madron is being honoured once again

Many sacred springs in Brigit's Isles are dedicated to the Goddess. The wonderful Nonita's or St. Non's Well, near to St. David's in West Wales is one. According to legend Nonita was a young nun who was raped by Sanctus, the king of Ceredigion, in a field on a high cliff next to the sea, which today contains the remains of a stone circle. The

110

Above left: Mother Nonita's or St Non's Well near St David's in west Wales.
Above right: Lovely statue of Mary the Mother Goddess looking towards St Non's Well

young nun who was virgin before this attack, continued through her pregnancy to live a life of chastity and poverty. When the child was due to be born she returned to the field where she had conceived. A violent storm was raging at the time which stilled into a summer's day when she arrived at the field. In the throes of childbirth Nonita supported herself on a stone which still bears the marks of her fingers, and broke in two in sympathy with her pain. At the moment of her son's birth a spring of the purest water burst from the earth to salute the Mother and her child, who later became St. David, the patron saint of Wales.

In 520 a chapel was built in the middle of the field where Nonita gave birth. A stone beneath the altar bears the marks of Nonita's fingers although some say these are traces of an Ogham inscription. Today St. Non's well lies in a beautiful location beside the field containing the ruins of the chapel and of a stone circle. Christian churches were often built on earlier sacred sites. Nearby is a Christian retreat centre which itself has a wonderful small chapel with a very feminine vibration. Here there are statues of the Mother Goddess Mary and stained glass windows depicting three Christianised Goddesses Bride (St. Brigit) , Nonita (St. Non) and Gwenhwyfar (St. Winifred).

Lady of the Lake

As Mother of Water the Lady of the South is also Lady of the Lake who is a familiar figure in the myths and legends of Britain and Europe. In their book *Ladies of the Lake* Caitlin and John Matthew name nine legendary women as Ladies of the Lake - Igraine, Guinevere, Morgan, Argante, Nimue or Vivienne, Enid, Kundry, Dindraine and Ragnell, who derive their powers from the Otherworld. Another ninefold Sisterhood is that of the Nine Morgens who rule over the Isle of Avalon surrounded by the Lake of Mysts. Their names were recorded by Geoffrey of Monmouth in the *Vita Merlini* in the twelfth century as Moronoe, Mazoe, Glitonea, Gliten, Cliton, Tyronoe, Thitis, Thetis and Morgen La Fey. There are other Lake women - the Giantess Cymeidi Cymeinfoll who emerged from an Irish lake to give birth to Irish and British warriors; the Maiden Liban; Meredith who guards the wells; the Damsels of the Well; and the Lady of the Fountain.

One of Her most well-known appearances is as Nelferch, the Lady of Llyn Y Fan Fach, a lake high in the Carmarthen Fans in South Wales. In legend a beautiful, mysterious Lady appeared to a young man, gliding over the surface of the lake. After several fruitless attempts to woo Her, She finally agreed to marry and stay with him until he gave Her three causeless blows. After many happy years together and giving birth to three sons, this happened accidentally and the Lady returned into the lake. She came back later to teach their sons the secrets of herbal medicine. Their descendants became famous as the Healers of Myddfai. The whole tale and the physician's remedies can be found in *The Herbal Remedies of the Physicians of Myddfai* edited by Dr Derek Bryce.

Llyn y Fan Fach, now a reservoir, is a beautiful Lake surrounded by high cliffs on three sides - see colour page next to page 85. The presence of the Lady can be felt here. The Physician's Meadow where the Lady taught Her sons about herbal medicine lies a distance away, covered in herbs and magic mushrooms when we visited.

The High Fruitful Mother

Hail, Mother Nature,
Creatrix of the world
Yours is the golden cloak
Covering all the earth

Birthgiving Serpent,
Dragon with a Womb
Queen Mother of Avebury
And Avalon

Cow Mother Madron,
Wetnurse to the worlds
Yours is the clear milk
Flowing from the wells

Fruitful Lammas Lady,
Goddess of the Grain
Ker is the Corn Mother
Riding on the Wain

Spinner of the threads,
Return to us each year
Holy Mother Ana
Weave your shining Web

The High Fruitful Mother Goddess reigns supreme. Whole unto Herself She is the Great Mother from whom all life is born. Self-created She carries the Universe in Her Virgin Womb and gives birth to the stars. She is the Weaver of the Web of Life and Time, spun from Her fertile Essence into the patterns of Her Nature. She is Mother of all the plants and animals. Her colour is the golden yellow of ripening grain.

To express the different qualities of the High Fruitful Mother Goddess in Brigit's Isles I would like to introduce two Goddesses whose

Opposite: Lammas Mother Goddess of the Grain by Willow Roe

names are not so well known as others, but whose presence is marked in ancient neolithic Womb/Tomb mounds, in the art of sacred landscape, in the names of sacred springs and in Lammas rites found throughout Britain and Europe from the earliest times.

She is the ancient Mother Goddess Madron and She is the Grain Goddess Ker.

Madron, Mother Goddess

The chapel at Madron's Well, near Madron, Cornwall

As Madron or Modron She is the Mother of Life, the bounteous Mother of All. Water flows out through openings in Her body from Her internal depths and Her life-renewing and healing qualities are remembered at holy wells and springs throughout Britain.

Madron's Well lies a mile or so outside the small Cornish town of Madron and is approached along a hawthorn lined track. Water from the well still flows through the ruined wellhouse.

Madron, the Bountiful Cow Mother

In Britain Madron, Brigit in Her Mother aspect, is the white, horned, red-eared Cow Mother who was revered throughout the ancient world as the Creatrix of the universe, which She curdled into shape from Her cow's milk. To the Egyptians She was Hathor with Her cow's head who daily gave birth to the sun. As Isis/Sothis Her soul was said to rest in the star Sirius. As Madron Her most common representation in Britain shows the womanly figure of the Goddess holding a cornucopia - a cow's horn, filled with fruit, grains and bread.

In Native American tradition the cow is equated to the buffalo. It was White Buffalo Calf Woman who brought the secrets of the smoking of the Pipe of Peace to the native peoples. She was said to have brought this knowledge from the Pleiades, the Seven Sisters who perch on the shoulder of the constellation of Taurus the Cow/Bull or Great White Buffalo. On the Sacred Wheel of Brigit Ana, Madron lies in the southwest, the direction on the Native American Wheel of the Great Sleeper Dreamer - She in whose dream we are living as She lies sleeping.

At Avebury from c.4,000-1,200 BCE the constellation of Taurus led by the Pleiades, rose due west of the central henge on the evening of the spring equinox. In early Zodiacs Taurus is the first sign of the year. The appearance of the bright yellow Alcyone of the Pleiades heralded the beginning of springtime. In India Alcyone is known as Amba, the Mother (*Star Names, Their Lore and Meaning*, R H Allen.)

Madron is the Provider, Nurturer and Protector. Like Brigit, She has a green cloak which covers the surface of the land. She is the bountiful Mother who gives the fruits of Her Earthly Body for the wellbeing of all living creatures. She is the Dea Nutrix, the Mother breast-feeding two babies, one at each breast. She is the wet-nurse to humanity.

Dea Matronae

Madron is a Triple Mother Goddess and often appears as three similarly clothed female figures known to the Kelts and Romans as the Dea Matronae. These three Goddesses each carry overflowing baskets or cornucopia - cow's or ram's horns filled with Nature's produce. They are often accompanied by coiled or rising serpents. These sculptures have been found all over Britain, often near to sacred wells. One found near to a spring at Cirencester shows three Goddesses with baskets of

Diana Griffiths

The Goddess with cornucopia - a cow's horn filled with grains and the fruits of the harvest.

Dea Nutrix: Mother Goddess feeding twins

Dea Matronae with baskets of produce and rising serpents found near a spring at Cirencester by Diana Griffiths

bread and fruit in their laps and serpents rising between their legs.

From the earliest times serpents have been associated with the Mother Goddess. The 30,000 year old child's grave at Mal'ta near Lake Baikal in Siberia, contained 20 Goddess figurines and an ivory plaque with a sevenfold spiral on one side and on the other three cobra-like snakes. Twisting snakes are inscribed on the stones of many neolithic mounds symbolising running water, rivers and creativity. In dreams snakes represent the regenerative powers of the Self and they have always played an important role in mythology from the Garden of Eden back to their earlier meaning as transforming chthonic powers.

Modron Verch Avallach

In the Welsh Triads the Mother Goddess was known as Modron verch Avallach, that is, Modron or Madron from the lineage of Avallach (*Trioedd Ynys Prydein* edited by Rachel Bromwich). Avallach was said to be a male ancestor from the Isle of Avalon, where Nine Sisters preside over the miraculously fertile Isle of Apples. Modron was said to be his daughter. I believe it is more likely, since Avalon was a Land of Women, that Modron was actually Mother of the lineage of Avallach and I claim Her as such. In later Arthurian legends Morgen la Fey was identified with Modron, but was actually Her daughter.

Madron's Talismans - Loom and Shuttle

Diana Griffiths

Madron is the Weaver who weaves the Threads of Life and Fate which the Maiden Goddess has spun on Her Spindle. Her talismans are the Loom on which the Threads of Life and Fate are anchored and the Shuttle which flies back and forth between the threads creating the fabric of life in this world.

Like the Spindle the Loom and Shuttle are both sacred symbols and practical objects. The Loom is the feminine anchor while the Shuttle represents the masculine potency moving back and forth between the threads, separating and binding the warp and weft of life together.

The Loom and Shuttle are elements in the fourfold cycle of Brigit

Two sides of the 30,000 year old Ma'alta plaque with seven circuit spiral and serpents

Ana. The other elements are Rhiannon's Comb which gathers and aligns the threads of wool and life, Brigit's Spindle or Spinning Wheel which spins the Thread of Life into balls of wool, and the Crone's Scissors or Sickle which cuts the threads at death.

Mother Wombs of Wood and Earth

In prehistoric times ceremonial buildings were constructed to reflect the shape of the Mother Goddess's body, particularly Her Womb and pregnant Belly. Early structures made of wood were circular buildings with domed thatched roofs. All that remains of these today are the postholes in the ground used for the roof supports, but their construction and shapes have been imaged by archaeologists. Inside they were dark and womb-like with circles of wooden pillars supporting a sloping circular roof. The original wooden structure built at the Sanctuary in Avebury is believed to have had such a shape.

Entrance passage into the dark inner Womb chamber of West Kennet long barrow near Avebury

High Fruitful Mother

The Kogi of Columbia, who still worship the Great Mother and believe themselves to be the Elder Brothers of the human race, still live and perform their ceremonies in dark, round, womb-like wooden structures - Wombs of the Earth Mother.

Many of the earth and stone monuments of the neolithic era dating from 4,500BCE were built in the shape of the Goddess's body. Round mounds were shaped like the pregnant Womb of the Great Mother. Long barrows were shaped like Her body. Inside both narrow vaginal passageways lead to one or several small dark womb-like chambers. Although these mounds which contain some human remains are now called burial chambers they are much more than this, representing the swollen pregnant body of the Mother Goddess to whom we return at death and from which we will all once again be reborn. Madron is the Mother of Death and also of Rebirth.

Many Native American *kivas* or sacred spaces were also round and carved or built into the earth. Entrance to the chambers was through a small cervical opening.

The Mother Goddess at Avebury

The great complex of stone circles and avenues at Avebury are claimed by many to represent a huge Serpent lying in the landscape. Its head is found at the Sanctuary. Its body is created by the standing stones of West Kennet Avenue, which pass through the great central henge of Avebury, and continue along the now underground Beckhampton Avenue. The serpent's tail coils, according to the dowser Brian Ashley, in the earthworks at Knoll Down. Similar representations of the Earth Serpent are found at Serpent Mound in Ohio, USA, built by the early Native Americans. It has been suggested that the two stone circles and avenues at Shap in Westmoorland are the remains of another landscape serpent.

Another interpretation of Avebury's arrangement of stones and mounds is that the Sanctuary and Knoll Down circles represent the Goddess's Ovaries. West Kennet and Beckhampton Avenues are Her Fallopian tubes, which come together in Her Womb/Cervix at the great central henge of Avebury, with its two internal rings of stones. This is a representation of the reproductive organs of the Great Mother. Silbury Hill which lies to the south, midway between the Sanctuary and Knoll Down, is the Goddess's visibly pregnant belly.

High Fruitful Mother

The Mother's fertile conceptual energies would be aroused and celebrated at appropriate times of the year, such as Beltane. According to Michael Dames, these generative organs lie within the body of a huge landscape Goddess, whose outline is marked by the positions of long barrows, stone circles and hill tops, stretching from the Vale of Pewsey across the whole Avebury complex to Temple Bottom. Michael Dames is the author of two wonderful Goddess books on Avebury - *The Avebury Cycle* and *Silbury Treasure*.

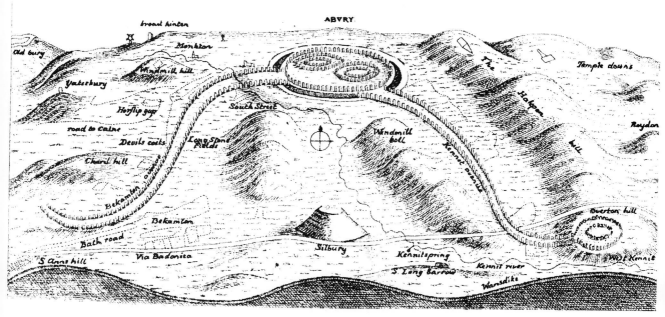

Viewed from the north looking south the whole arrangement of stones and avenues also appears as the head of a horned animal - a Sacred Cow or Bull. The avenues are the horns while the central henge is the head with two eyes. Silbury Hill is the crowning thousand petalled lotus above the head. In the great Kretan civilisation of the Goddess, cow's horns also represented both the Fallopian tubes and the Womb of the Goddess.

This multiple vision of Cow, Snake and Womb was a major feature in many neolithic sites. Their complementary nature meant that they could be used for rituals which invoked both Goddess and God, which were meaningful to both women and men. Michael Dames has suggested that at Avebury at the appropriate season great crowds of people would move down both avenues, women from the Sanctuary and men from the Knoll, to meet and join at the central henge.

Serpent/Womb/Cow Horn symbolism within the Avebury complex. From an engraving by the 18th century antiquarian Dr William Stuckley.

121

Silbury Hill – The Lammas Mother

Madron is the creative and nurturing Womb whom the neolithic peoples honoured in the shapes of the sacred mounds which they built. Silbury Hill in Wiltshire is the highest and best known example of the Mother's Womb in Britain, rising to 130ft. It was built circa 2750 BCE some time before the standing stones of the Avebury complex were erected c.2,600 BCE. The builders of Avebury obviously took into account the position of Silbury Hill during their erection of the henge

The Mother Womb of Silbury Hill viewed from the east. Photo by Roland Pargeter.

*Silbury Mother Womb
by Marian Elliott*

and avenues of standing stones, erecting the main circle to the north. The pregnant Womb of Silbury lies in a direct line between the two ovaries of the Sanctuary and Knoll Down and is visible from both. It gives a vision of the aim of union and provides a signalling point for the timing of ceremonies.

Silbury Hill is now covered with grasses and on its slopes wheat and barley grow. From the top the Lammas Sun can be seen setting over Knoll Down as the Full Moon rises opposite it over the Sanctuary,. In its original unclothed chalk form Silbury Hill would have appeared as

High Fruitful Mother

a great white Womb in the landscape, gleaming in the golden light of the sun, hauntingly beautiful in the silver light of the moon. Truly a vision to behold!

According to Michael Dames in his inspired book *The Silbury Treasure*, Silbury Hill is the Womb of the pregnant Mother Goddess at Lammas. The shape of the Mother can be seen where the chalk used to build Silbury was carved out of the surrounding land. This depression often fills with water. In ancient times at Lammas the Goddess appeared to give birth to the full moon, as it reflected in the water surrounding the mound. Although strenuous efforts have been made by archaeologists to find a burial chamber for a King within Silbury Hill, none has been found and its original veneration as the Womb of the Harvest Mother is returning.

The Dragon Path

St Michael's Mount in Cornwall where the Mary/Michael Dragon Line comes to land from the sea.

Hamish Miller and Paul Broadhurst in their fascinating dowsing odyssey *The Sun and the Serpent*, trace the serpentine pathways of the Dragon Path as it travels across the southern half of Britain. The Mary and Michael earth currents intertwine like the two serpents on a caduceus, around the straight central Dragon line. The Michael line passes

through high places and churches dedicated to St Michael and the Mary line passes through wells and valleys and St Mary's churches. The central Dragon line emerges from the sea at St Michael's Mount in Cornwall, travelling over the moors of Cornwall and Devon to Glastonbury and then to Avebury and on to Bury St Edmund's and out into the North Sea.

Where the Mary and Michael lines meet and entwine there are strong energy vortices, like the chakras in the human body, which have been honoured since ancient times as power centres. The two most obvious are Avebury and Glastonbury. It is at such places that the veils between the worlds are thin and cosmic and earth energies pour in at particular times of the year. The axis of the Dragon line is oriented to sunrise at Beltane and Lammas, and sunset at Imbolc and Samhain. As the sun rises in the east over the end of the Dragon line in the North Sea all the places on the line are energised by the sun's physical and psychic rays. This is one of the reasons it is good to visit these sacred sites at Beltane and Lammas.

The Mother Goddess at Glastonbury/Avalon

The body of the Mother Goddess is also visible in the landscape of the Isle of Avalon, one of the great spiritual centres of Brigit's Isles.

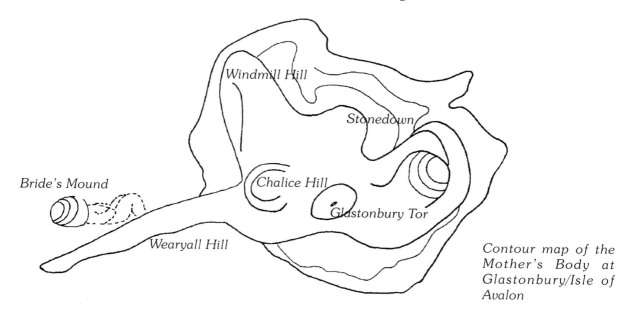

Contour map of the Mother's Body at Glastonbury/Isle of Avalon

High Fruitful Mother

Here the outline of Her birth-giving body can be traced in the physical contours of the land. A Giantess, She lies upon Her back with Glastonbury Tor as Her left breast, Her right breast slipping over onto Paradise Lane. Her head lies back into the earth at Stonedown. Wearyall Hill is Her outstretched left leg, its foot submerging into the earth beside Bride's Mound. Windmill Hill is Her right leg tucked beneath Her body. Chalice Hill is Her pregnant belly and as the Mother Goddess She continually gives birth to the town of Glastonbury and all that happens there, and to the Maiden Brigit and the Salmon of Wisdom at Bride's Mound, which lies between Her outstretched legs at Beckery. (*In the Nature of Avalon*, Kathy Jones).

Lammas Festival of the Mother Goddess

The bounteousness of the High Fruitful Mother Goddess is celebrated at Lammas, the third of the four crossquarter fire festivals of the year, which is dedicated to the Pregnant and Birthgiving Mother Goddess of Nature. Lammas comes at 15 degrees Leo around August 6th or 7th. It is commonly celebrated at the end of July and beginning of August. Lammas falls halfway between the Summer Solstice and the Autumn Equinox and in Brigit's Isles comes between the hay and wheat harvests.

The name Lammas comes from the Saxon *Hlaf-mass*, the Feast of Bread and is a celebration of the produce of the grain. In Brigit's Isles it comes at the height of the summer when flowers are blooming and all the fruits and grains are swelling and ripening ready for harvesting. Young animals and birds grow in strength. It is a Festival of the fertility of the Mother Goddess as She gives birth.

This Festival of fruitfulness became identified with the Keltic midsummer festival of Lughnasadh, which celebrated the cutting of the corn and the death and resurrection of the God Lugh or Llud or Nudd as the Grain God or Corn King. Reminders of this festival of mourning for the death of the Corn King continue to the present day in Wakes Weeks, when annual summer holidays are traditionally taken by many Northern and Midlands factories. Wakes Weeks are holy-days in which family Ancestors are remembered and their graves or homes visited on holiday.

In the Goddess tradition at Lammas we honour the Abundant High Fruitful Mother Goddess and celebrate the many facets of Her creative expression at the Glastonbury Goddess Conference.

The Mysteries of Eleusis

In ancient Greece the Eleusinian Mysteries celebrated the transformation cycle of the Grain Goddess, which is mirrored in the vegetation cycle of spring, summer, autumn and winter. The Goddesses Demeter or Ceres, Persephone or Kore, Hecate and Pluto all played a part. The Mysteries re-enacted the tale of annual descent in the autumn to meet the Underworld Goddess followed by the rebirth of Life and Nature in springtime. The most sacred moment of the Eleusinian Mysteries was the revelation of the Kore as an ear of corn.

At some time in history Pluto's original feminine gender was stripped from Her and Pluto became Hades, a male God rather than an Underworld Goddess. Hades was said to have forcibly abducted Kore against Her will as she picked flowers in a meadow and then raped Her. Later after She had spent some time with him so the story went, She came to love Him. This was part of the male fantasy that male violence somehow leads to love.

This was a reversal of an earlier myth in which fascination with the Self (narcissus), leads to the ground opening up beneath one's feet and a falling into the shadowy Underworld. It is only through this descent that the personal and collective Shadow can be redeemed and integrated. Astrologically Pluto is the powerful outer planet whose transit of a natal chart represents an encounter with the transforming Underworld Goddess.

Modern day statue of Demeter with Her sheaf of grains

The British Myth Cycle of Ker

I shall retell this ancient tale of initiation into the Mysteries of the Grain in Brigit's Isles translating the names and stories of the Greek and Kretan Goddesses into those of our own British ancestors. The myth cycle reflects the changing seasons of the year.

One day the beautiful Maiden Kernel is in the meadow picking flowers for her Mother, the Grain Goddess Ker's altar. She bends down to look at a particularly beautiful Narcissus. Entranced by its glowing colour she gazes into the flower which reflects her own beauty and time passes. As she looks the earth begins to shake and the ground opens up beneath her feet. Kernel tumbles into a deep Underworld chasm which closes over her head. She screams, but no-one hears her. She is on the ground and can see nothing. Its completely dark. Unhurt physically she gets to her feet and feels around her with her hands. She is very frightened. She moves slowly forward feeling her way in the darkness, not knowing where she is going, afraid of what she may bump into or fall down. All she can hear is the pounding of her heart and her own fast breaths. She stops and strains to listen. Ahead of her in the darkness she hears a faint sound. She moves slowly towards it.

Ahead she begins to discern a glimmer of light which grows as she walks towards it. She senses that she is walking along a tunnel and then as the light increases she sees its floor, ceiling and walls. She is comforted by being able to see her surroundings a little. The sound gets louder, a bubbling sound. The tunnel is long but eventually she reaches the end and emerges into a great dark red cavern. Deep in the bottom of the cavern she sees the source of light that has sustained her on her journey.

A fire burns in the earth and on the fire is a Cauldron in which a liquid bubbles. Beside the cauldron sits a great White Sow-like Hag. This is the awesome figure of Kernel's Grandmother, Keridwen and this cavern in the earth is her domain. Kernel is even more frightened. She has never been down into Keridwen's Underworld before. She has never seen such an ugly old woman.

Kernel stands very still hoping Keridwen won't notice she's there, but her Grandmother turns towards her and grunting like a Sow beckons Kernel towards the fire. Kernel wants to run but behind her all is darkness. She walks slowly towards her Grandmother and trembling with fear her legs give way beneath her. She sits on the ground beside the fire, the cauldron and her Grandmother, and unable to hide her emotions any longer cries and shakes the fear out of her body. When her tears subside she falls into a deep and dreamless sleep.

Sometime later Kernel wakens. As she sees the fire and the round shape of her Grandmother, her fear rises again. Keridwen hands her a cup of warm liquid from her cauldron, sweet to the taste and refreshing, Kernel calms a little. Over the next hours, days and weeks Kernel sits beside the fire and beside Keridwen, drinking from the cauldron. Its taste changes daily from sweet to strong to sour and back. Too scared to talk Kernel watches her Grandmother as she tends her cauldron, and learns to listen.

As time goes by Kernel gradually becomes accustomed to the moods and ways of her Grandmother. She learns not to flinch at her

High Fruitful Mother

Willow Roe

Keridwen, the Great White Sow Grandmother
Grandmother's grunting voice. She learns to sit with her fear, with her grief, anger and pain and each day she helps feed the fire with sticks. The fire that heats her Grandmother's Cauldron of Regeneration and Inspiration. Over time she comes to appreciate her Grandmother's ways..

Meanwhile back in the Middleworld above ground Kernel's Mother the Grain Goddess Ker, is in deep mourning for the disappearance of her daughter Kernel. Winter descends on the earth and all vegetation dies. The earth hardens and nothing grows.

The myth cycle of Ker, Kernel, Keridwen and Kerhiannon by Marian Elliott

After long months of waiting and no word from her favourite daughter, Ker asks her sister Kerhiannon, who is able to travel between the worlds, to search for Kernel in the Underworld. Kerhiannon enters the Underworld via a secret opening within the Hollow Hills. As she journeys down into the earth the inner radiance from her body lights her way through the darkness. She follows the Underworld pathways to the Red Cavern and finds Kernel there helping her Grandmother. The Sun-fire light of Kerhiannon's golden presence reminds Kernel of the delights of the Middleworld and she longs to return to her mother Ker above ground. She turns to say goodbye to Keridwen and realises how much she has learned from her Dark Grandmother and how much she loves her. She promises that for three months each year she will return to sit with Keridwen in the darkness and help feed the fire and drink from her cauldron.

As she leaves Keridwen gives Kernel one last drink from her cauldron. The taste is amazing unlike anything she has tasted before.

The germ of her life quickens and begins to grow once again. Imbued with energy and creativity Kernel returns with Kerhiannon to the Middleworld. Ker is overjoyed to see her and her Nature blossoms forth once more in the celebration of Springtime. The cycle of the seasons continues. There is joy in the Middleworld the following Lammas when Ker gives birth to a new Kernababy, a new Kernel.

This cycle of the Grain was celebrated throughout the ancient world in one form or another from the earliest times, in the Mysteries of Inanna, Ishtar, Ker, Kore, Ceres, etc.. It is one of the primary initiatory rites into the Mysteries of the Feminine, revealed through descent to the Underworld Goddess and retreat within to face the inner and outer darkness. If survived it can lead to integration of the personal shadow, to wholeness and unlimited creativity.

Sacred Sites of Ker in Brittany

The name of the Goddess Ker appears most frequently in the place names of the many neolithic sacred sites found in Brittany and Northern France. Some of the most important and well preserved lie in the region of Carnac, with its great temple complex and long parallel lines of standing stones. They include Kermario, Kerlescan, Kercado, Kergonan and Kerleven. The translation from the Breton says that *Ker* means *place* or *of the dwarfs*. Dwarfs are Otherworldly peoples dedicated to the Goddess and invisible to mortal eyes, indicating the allegiance of these neolithic sites to the Grain Goddess Ker.

The People Who Erected the Standing Stones

In folklore the Korrs or   are the dwarfs who first brought the standing stones to Brittany and Cornwall. They were so strong they could carry the massive stones on their backs. They now live in caves hidden lives beneath dolmens and standing stones, and below sea level. They are one to three feet tall with hunched bodies, black skin, dark shaggy hair and bright red eyes. They are prophets and magicians and know where treasure is hidden. They love to dance inside stone circles but only at night when the grass burns in circles under their feet.

High Fruitful Mother

The old Korred include the Corics, Kerions, Kouricans, Kourils, Korandon and Crions. The Crions can laugh all night as they watch dancing humans die of exhaustion. The early Phoenicians who sailed to Brittany brought with them the Couretes or Carikines, who intermarried to become Corriquets, Korriks and Kornikaned, who carry small horns attached to their belts. It is fascinating that these names are all related both to Ker and to the erectors of the standing stones.

In a healing ceremony Pauline immerses herself in the freezing waters of St Cybi's (Ker's) healing well at Llangybi in North Wales, which is said to contain a sacred eel, the Korrigan of the well

Korrigans are Fountain Women who live in underground caves, but spend their waking hours near the sacred springs and fountains that are found next to standing stones and dolmens. Korrigans are awesome diaphanous creatures with long golden hair which shines at night. They are shape shifters and can appear as spiders, eels or snakes. Their secret rituals change springs into healing wells. In Brigit's Isles many healing wells were said to contain a sacred eel, the Korrigan of the well.

When the moon is full Korrigan comb their hair with golden combs and then bathe in the cool spring waters. They can be seen without harm by human women, but if a man sees one he is bound to marry her within three days or die. At Imbolc they have a festival at which they drink to the secret of poetry and earthly wisdom from a crystal goblet. They are said to be the granddaughters of nine holy druidesses of ancient Gaul, a synonym for the ninefold Goddess of the ancient world. (*A Field Guide to the Little People* by Nancy Arrowsmith)

In neolithic and historical time there was a strong connection between Brittany or little Britain and Brigit's Isles. Our neolithic Ancestors who brought the secrets of the grain and standing stones to Britain had come north and westwards from France and Spain, bringing with them their ancient divinities. The Korres migrated to Cornwall where they became known as Spriggans.

Ker in Brigit's Isles

In Brigit's Isles the name Ker appears in several important place names including Kerswell, Kernow (the Cornish name for Cornwall), Keredigion/Cardigan including part of Wales now lying beneath the Irish sea, and County Kerry in Ireland. Other variations of Her name are found in the ancient sacred sites of Carn Brea, Carn Euny, Cardiff, Cornwall, Callanish, Caerleon, Caernarfon, Caermarthen, all the mythic Caer Sidi's or glass castles, Cerne Abbas, Callanish, Castle Cary, Clava Cairns, Cerrig Duon, Corbridge, Cumbria, Corrimony and Carlisle

Corn Circles

Over the last 15 years or so Ker has been making Her presence felt in the regular appearance of Crop Circles in grain fields in southern

Part of the central crop circle surrounded by six smaller circles that appeared at Butleigh Wooton nr Glastonbury in 1990. It was noticed when deer were seen within it in the corner of a field.

Britain. Simple and complex circular formations have appeared in all kinds of crops including wheat and barley, each May, June, July and August. So far all attempts to explain their mystery have been unsuccessful. Apart from those made by landscape artists, circle creators may be space beings, tiny balls of light or the Grain Mother Herself may be speaking to us in symbols and signs.

Other Names of Ker

In other forms Ker was also Kele, Kale the Giantess or Kali the Great Mother. In Ireland a Kele-de was named as a Bride (from Brigit) of God. The Culdees were holy men dedicated to the Goddess Kele. The Gaulish Carnutes were descended from the Goddess Car. In Irish legend, Carman was a Goddess who was brought to Ireland by three powerful magicians from Persia, which was then known as Carmania and lay in the Fertile Crescent region where grain is believed to have first been cultivated.

In ancient Greece the seven Caryatids were known as the Mothers of the World. They were the earthly representations of the seven Sisters of the Pleiades. The Caryatids are butterflies, ancient symbols of regeneration and transformation, inscribed on early Kretan seals and wall paintings.

Karuna

One of the main identifications of Ker as the Mother Goddess is revealed in the tantric term *karuna*, which signifies *mother love*, directly experienced in infancy and expanded in adulthood to embrace all forms of loving including the sexual and erotic. The sacred whores of the Mother Goddess gave men the experience of the Mother's *karuna*, which was later purged of its sexual connotation to become *caritas* - charity. Tantric sages of the east claim that *karuna* is the essence of all religion.

Kauri or Brilliant One was the Dakini who dispensed *karuna* to the gods through Her sacred Yoni, imaged as a cowrie shell. Cowrie shells have represented the Goddess from the earliest times. In 20,000 BCE they were used to decorate the bodies of the Ancestors. In 7,000 BCE in Jericho, they were placed over the eyes of the dead. In Buddhist paintings large cowrie shells hold the blood of life and death and *amrita* or the nectar of immortality. In Africa they are symbols of wealth.

Ker the Deer Mother

As well as being the Grain Goddess, I believe that Ker is also the Deer Mother, the primeval Birthgiving Goddess, who is the partner of the Stag God Kernunnos. Her image is preserved in Scottish and Irish fairy tales of women who would transform themselves into deer, and in deer who turned into women. This may also be a memory of the shamanka who donned deerskins as she journeyed in the Mystery Rites of the Grain Goddess. It was believed that the Greek Goddess Artemis could change into the form of a deer and statues of Her were clothed in deerskins. The Sumerian Goddess of childbirth was a horned deer.

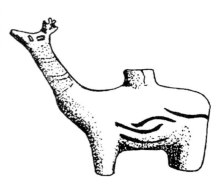

A ritual vase in the shape of the Deer Mother from Bulgaria 5000BCE

Kernunnos

In terms of mythical revelation, the male partner to Ker was the Stag God Kernunnos or Cernunnos, whose initiatory rites reveal the Mysteries of the Divine Masculine. Diana Griffiths and I sat with the Deer and the Whale Keeper of ancient memory to retrieve fragments of his mythic teachings..

Kernunnos is depicted on the silver Gundestrop Cauldron found in a Jutland peat bog, dating from 300 BCE. He is seated cross-legged with Stag's horns on His head. In his left hand he holds a snake and in his right hand a torc or bracelet. He is surrounded by the animals of the forest and a small person riding on the back of a whale.

What is not usually mentioned about this beautifully decorated cauldron are the many images of the Goddess also found upon it. She is depicted as the nurturing Mother with hands on Her breasts and the torc around Her neck, which only She can give and which must be won by those human men who aspire to claim their Godhead. She also appears as the Lady of the Beasts and as Goddess of Death and Rebirth.

Representations of the Stag God are found from the earliest times in cave paintings in Italy (Val Camonica, 3000 BCE), Spain and in France (the Wizard of Les Trois Freres, Ariege, c. 13000 BCE). These paintings represent the totemic nature of the stag and the taking on of his spirit by the Shaman.

Image on the silver Gundestrop Cauldron showing Kernunnos with horns, torc, snake and deer by Diana Griffiths

The Myth Cycle of Kernunnos

The Stag Man God from La Pileta, Spain, 13,000BCE by Diana Griffiths

As in Ker's story, there are four characters in the British myth cycle of Kernunnos - the Red Stag, Herne the Hunter, Kernunnos and the Green Man, who come to prominence in turn at the solstices and equinoxes rather than the crossquarter festivals. They reflect the special relationship between men and animals and the masculine path of initiation through the inspiration of the spirit of the animals. Their story emphasises men's responsibility to be the protectors of Nature.

Through the winter the Green Man of the forests protects the family of the Red Deer. Beneath his evergreen branches he hides the does and young deer, and the stags with their branching horns which are beginning to show signs of wear and tear. Protected from the winter storms they find food beneath the trees. Snow falls softly covering their tracks. In winter the forest is silent, in repose, in retreat.

We celebrate the life of the Green Man and Green Lady at Winter Solstice when we bring evergreen trees into every British home, decorating them with lights and sparkling treasures as Xmas trees. We honour them at midwinter when nothing green except the evergreen trees grows in the land.

Slowly as the season turns the Sun Goddess's rays once again begin to penetrate the dark woods, warming the earth, quickening the seeds that lie dormant in the ground. The Red Stag stays in the forest and sheds the antlers which have served him in the previous year.

As Spring Equinox approaches around March 21st, day and night become equal in length. The Stag emerges from the forest to climb the mountains. The sap rises in the trees and plants, and sexual energy awakens in all the nature realms. The first branches of the Stag's new horns begin to grow and he starts to listen to the sounds of the cosmos.

At Beltane the does hide beneath the Green Man's coat in the woods and give birth to the young they have carried through the winter. During summer the does and young deer travel together. The stags lead more solitary lives and through the summer grow branching horns, symbols of their power, age and strength, antennae to the stars.

On Midsummer's Eve from the forest, straight and tall like a tree, emerges Herne the Hunter with his Dogs. He is searching for the Stag who will renew his divine power. In July and August the stags rub their antlers against the branches of the trees. The velvety coating that has protected their new horns as they grow, falls off and their horn strengthen.

Herne searches for the King Stag who will be in his prime just as the rutting season begins. He makes forays tinto the forest in search of his prize.

Just before Autumn Equinox at last his hounds come upon the Stag standing majestically on a rocky crag. They rush to the King Stag and drag him to the ground. Herne runs after and makes the kill. Taking the Horns from the Stag he places them upon his own brow and is thereby transformed. He takes on the Stag's wild spirit, his divinity. He becomes Kernunnos, the Stag Godman, and bellows his delight. Although untried as yet, he knows himself to be strong, maybe stronger than all the rest. He draws the fertile hinds to him and tests himself against his brothers. He locks horns with his fellow Stags and inspired by the God, he can overcome all his rivals. He is Lord of the Forest.

The Stag/God/Man Kernunnos by David Dunger

As Kernunnos he reigns throughout the autumn. Filled with the wild spirit of the Stag in his prime he has his choice of the does, drawn by his animal magnetism. Beltane will be the season of celebration for the offspring of these unions. They will all return one day to challenge him. The wounds he then receives will bring him true wisdom.

This spirit of the God is not constant, but like human sperm must be continually reproduced. Kernunnos cannot keep the divine Stag horns for longer than a season. With the passing of the winter solstice he must shed his horns and return them back to the Earth. As with the grinding of Ker's grain to make flour, the Horns of Kernunnos must also be ground down, to become fertilising spirit, spread upon the Earth, regenerating the soil. (Rudolph Steiner, the Founder of Anthroposophy, claimed the best fertiliser is ground down stag's horn.)

Bareheaded Kernunnos returns to the forest and clothing himself in leaves and branches, he merges into the woodland once more. He becomes the Green Man. Does and young deer and other creatures shelter from the harsh wintry elements and dangers of life beneath his evergreen branches. He is the Provider and Protector of wild animals. Through the winter the animals will live safely, re-emerging once again with the coming of the Spring

The myth cycle of Kernunnos points to a way of being for men which allows for the expression of power and strength, while returning to the Earth what She needs to sustain all the forms of life which live upon Her body. The great benefits of spirit must not just stay in the realms of the head and mind, but must be spread down to the heart and back to the earth.

Mother of Earth
Brigantia, Banbha, Gaia

The Mother of Earth in the West is Brigantia, Goddess of the land which includes all of the pre-Keltic empire of Brigit's Isles, as well as Brittany in northwestern France and western Spain, when they were recognised as one whole ruled by the Goddess. She is also Banba, Lady of the Land from before the Flood, Ertha, Queen of the Earth and Gaia our Mother Earth.

Brigantia is the Earth in which all of our nature finds its roots and sustenance. She is the Land on which we live, where we are creative and manifest our innermost dreams. She is the Place where our ancestors came from, where they lived and died, where we live and die. She is the Land that we call Home, where we feel welcome, nurtured, where something heartfelt opens within us each time we return to Her. She is the Earth where our cultural and familial roots lie deep in the Soil itself. If we or our forebears have moved away from Her to live in other places in the world at some time we need to return to Her, to reconnect the broken strand in our lives, in order to feel whole.

Opposite: the form of the Goddess can be seen in the natural contours of the landscape of Glastonbury/Avalon. Glastonbury Tor at the top of the picture is the Mother Goddess's left breast.

She is the Ground we walk upon with every footstep. In many places Her physical form is visible in the very outline of hills and valleys. Here are Her breasts, there Her pregnant belly or Her head with flowing hair and there Her limbs. One such special place where the Goddess can be seen is on the Isle of Avalon at Glastonbury. Here Her shape as Maiden Swan, Mother Goddess and Crone can be traced in the contours of the landscape. (See *In the Nature of Avalon*, Kathy Jones)

Brigantia is connected to Brigit and some say She is the same Goddess. She was also known in Roman times as Britannia, both the land of Britain and the Goddess Brigit-Ana whose sacred wheel we honour in this book.

Mother of Earth

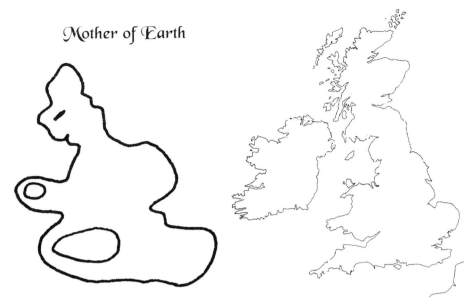

Abover right: Contour map of the Crone who rides upon the back of the Swan in Avalon.
Above left: Map of the land of Brigantia/Brigit's Isles

Below : a knot of wood replicates a sculpture of the Crone of Avalon by the author on the right

Brigantia is the Goddess who has just given birth to Her child and to the harvest. Her form can be seen in the contours of the land that includes modern day England, Scotland and Wales, with Ireland as Her child. This form is duplicated in miniature in the contours of the Goddess who rides on the back of the Swan upon the Isle of Avalon.

Banbha

The Earth Mother in the West is also Banbha, who is equated in Ireland with Kersair the early Grain Goddess. In the Irish *Book of Invasions* Banbha claimed to be older than Noah, coming from a time long before the great Flood which is mentioned in many ancient texts from around the world. Banba is identified with the land which sank beneath the waves during the Flood and later re-emerged from the sea. Ireland was known as the *island of Banbha of the Women* and the West is identified with women's mysteries and wisdom.

Talismans, Colours, Creatures of the West

Brigantia/Banbha's talismans are of the Earth. They include Stone which represents the Rock which is the backbone of the land; the Orb - a round ball which represents the globe of Planet Earth; and a sparkling Crystal, which grows in secret under fire and pressure within the darkness of the earth.

The colour of the West is orange/brown, the colours of nature and the earth in the autumn in Brigit's Isles, when the days begin to shorten in earnest and all of Her nature dies back to the earth. She is the glowing orange setting Sun as it prepares to journey below the horizon taking these islands into darkness. She is the waning Moon, letting go Her grip on the tides, turning away from brightness, moving into darkness. She is the Vernal Equinox, a liminal space when light and dark are held, for a short time, in equal measure, preparing us for the darkness of winter which later descends on the land.

The creatures of the West are the Boar, the Badger and the Fox. Wily, cunning creatures who hunt at eventide and dawn they become aggressive if cornered. Stories from folklore tell of the Fox who chases the Red Hen and the Hare of the Spring Equinox, describing the turning of the year.

The Art of Sacred Landscape

In Britain and Ireland the earliest beliefs about the Earth Goddess were expressed in the art of creating sacred landscape - in the correct positioning of mounds, stone circles and standing stones within an existing natural landscape; in their placement in relation to the underground currents of the Serpent Mother and to the physical contours of valleys, hills and mountains, rivers and streams; and the alignment of all these to the heavenly cycles of the sun, moon and stars. Our ancestors, the builders of the neolithic, had great knowledge of this art which we have almost completely lost or submerged into unconsciousness, occasionally getting it right by chance. Known to the Chinese as Feng Shui, these are the secrets of the Serpent and the Dragon Mothers of the Earth.

Circles of Wood

Many of the earliest sacred sites in Britain so far discovered were large rounded enclosures marked out by tall wooden posts and specially positioned within the natural landscape. Today there is nothing to see on the surface only postholes in the earth remain, but the posts themselves may have been carved like Native American totem poles or made from unworked wood. Remains of such circles have come to light in the last few years near Avebury in Wiltshire, in central Wales and at Stanton Drew in Somerset. Sea Henge, a beautiful small woodhenge dating from 4020BCE, recently emerged from beneath the shifting sands, partly submerged by the sea, at Holme next the Sea in Norfolk.

Stone Circles

Opposite above: the intimate stone circle of Derrintaggart West with sacred mountains beyond on the Bheara Peninsula, County Cork, Eire.
Below: Ardgroom Outside also on the Bheara Peninsula, surrounded by sea and mountains.

Some of the best examples of the art of sacred landscape can be seen in the placing of stone circles in relation to the surrounding countryside. Stone circles are not usually found as might be expected, on the tops of hills, but they almost always have a definite relationship to a neighbouring hill or hills and mountains. Stone circles are often positioned in the middle of a landscape bowl or cauldron, with a horizon of hills on three or more sides. Natural and artificial notches in the surrounding hills provide markers for the rising and setting of the sun, moon and stars at different seasons of the year.

Mother of Earth

The remains of great numbers of stone circles and stone rows are found all over Brigit's Isles and western Europe. Built from the late Neolithic into the Bronze age, they vary in size from intimate nine stone circles to large ceremonial sites with a hundred and more stones. They are sacred sites where the earth, the sky, the ancestors and the Goddess were honoured. Today people journey in their thousands to visit these sacred sites and experience the enigma that is the knowledge of the Earth Mother that our ancestors knew and we have forgotten.

As well as stone circles and stone avenues there are thousands of single megaliths dotted around the countryside. Some of these are directional markers to the rising and setting of the sun and moon. Others act like acupuncture needles helping the energy flow in Mother Earth's meridians.

Below: The great female megalith of Maen Llia is beautifully positioned lying north-south in the high river valley of Afon Llia in the desolate mountainous Fforest Fawr, west of the Brecon Beacons in Wales.

Ertha, Gaia

Other familiar names of the Earth Mother are Ertha, who gave Her name to the planet, and Gaia, the Greek Goddess who was remembered once again by the scientist James Lovelock. He named Her as the whole matrix of the interlocking systems of Nature which supports and maintains all life on earth. She is the Earth Mother and Mother of Earth.

Beautiful statue of Gaia created by Oberon Zell with the Earth as her pregnant belly and the evolutionary streams of plants and animals and sea creatures carved on Her body and in Her hair.

Opposite above: Ancient Futures. Painting by Katheryn Trenshaw Below: Mother of the Apple Isle. Painting by Jill Smith

The Crone Goddess

The Crone is craggy, old and wizened
A Straw-made Hag whose Famine is feared,
Her black rod smites the landscape
Like Bera's silver hammer
Which rings out the curses
Of death and decay in Her autumnal realm

The Toad She squats upon the ground
Her green wart-covered skin hangs down
Like Her Mother Lady Baubo
Sheela's legs are akimbo
Her dark red flesh parts
To reveal Her awesome Gig-Vulva

The Sow's white skin is cold and clammy
Deep in Her Underworld realm of death
No comfort here in folds of flesh
Hers is the Tomb/Womb
The end of incarnation in
Keridwen's Cauldron of Regeneration

The Grandmothers sit in their circles of silence
Maligned and forgot in the myths of our land
We didn't listen or heed to their wisdom
Yet they hold the Wise Blood
Within wombs that are withered
Filled with the gifts of Her mysteries

The fourth aspect of the ancient Goddess in Brigit's Isles is the Crone or Hag, known as the Old Woman, the Death Goddess, Dark Goddess, Queen of the Underworld and Grand Mother. After autumn leaves have turned to gold, orange and red upon the trees, the rich beauty of maturity begins to decay. Winds blow the leaves off the trees

Opposite: Crone Goddess by Willow Roe

151

revealing their wooden bones and the rains come. Death draws near and the Hag Goddess begins Her reign.

Her colour in the Northwest is Black and Her festival is known as Samhain, pronounced Sam- or Sow-ain. This is the Festival of the Goddess as the Great White Sow. Like the mother sow who may eat her own young the Sowain Mother eats up the souls of the dead placed in Her care. Samhain marks the end of the old Keltic Year and the beginning of a New Year.

We will explore three faces of the Crone Goddess to describe Her different qualities. These are the Bringer of Death who appears as both Hag and Old Woman; Sheela na Gig, whose blatant sexual image symbolises both death to the ego through sexual surrender and return to the Goddess through Her Yonic gate of death; and the Underworld Goddess Keridwen, Keeper of the Cauldron and Grand Mother of Death, Transformation, Inspiration and Regeneration.

Statuette of the Death Goddess by the author

The Bringer of Death

The Bringer of Death is one of the main forms of the Goddess revered by our early British ancestors and the majority of neolithic stone monuments were erected to honour the dead and to create sacred places in which people could communicate with their ancestors and with Her.

In the neolithic era life and death were intimately entwined. Human life was lived close to nature and was much more obviously concerned with physical survival than life is now in our modern Western world. There were dangerous wild animals in the forests and diseases like the plague, which could afflict whole societies, like the one which wiped out the early Irish people of Parthalon in a week. On the whole people lived much shorter lives than today, with most of their elders dying before the age of 40 years. The Bringer of Death like the Birth-giving Mother was revered for Her awesome powers.

The Long Barrows of the Death Mother

The Death Mother is represented in Brigit's Isles in the shape of the ritual mounds known as long barrows, which date from circa 4,250 BCE. She was the Tomb in which bodies and bones were buried at death, and the Womb from which all souls would one day be reborn. The long barrows were huge, long mounds of earth, shaped like Her body, often covered in gleaming white chalk or in stones with sparkling quartz crystal veins, or they may have been faced with wood, whose decorations we can only imagine. Many of them had horn-shaped forecourts in which the remains of fires, pottery, animal bones and horns are found.

Built c.3,250BCE West Kennet Long Barrow situated near to Avebury was originally 20 feet high, 80 feet wide and 326 feet long. It has a long spine of sandstone, like the spine in a human or animal body, which runs the length of the barrow. The spine is covered by a chalk mound which has a long ditch on either side where the chalk was dug from the ground. At the eastern end of the barrow there are beautiful stone lined tomb/womb chambers, where 46 bodies were found interred

Entrance forecourt of West Kennet Long Barrow near Avebury which was originally a curved arc of stones. The mound was filled with chalk rubble and blocked off with huge stones in 2,600BCE

153

as whole or partial skeletons. The inner chambers are shaped like the Goddess's squatting body as in the Maltese Goddess temples and the body of the barrow is aligned towards the Sanctuary on the horizon. It is one of many long barrows in the area which form the outline of Michael Dames' Goddess in the landscape.

West Kennet long barrow was used for ceremonies for several hundred years and then in 2,600BCE at the time when Avebury henge was erected, the inner chambers of the long barrow were filled with chalk and rubble, and huge blocking stones in the shape of a stone ox were placed across its entrance. A new people had arrived, perhaps the Tuatha De Danaan, who built in circles and came from the skies.

The entrances to the long barrows often face towards the east or south east, so that the rays of the rising winter sun or the full moon could flood the internal chamber. In ancient times the Moon was often associated with death, its waxing form being filled by the souls of the dead. Ancestors visited the earth from their lunar home travelling along the full moon beams into the long barrows, where they could then be contacted. West Kennet Long Barrow is still today a powerful and sacred place where we can feel the presence of our foremothers in the stillness within the mound.

Samhain

Samhain is now celebrated at the end of October and beginning of November, half way between the Autumn Equinox and the Winter Solstice. It is the Festival of the Death Mother and the Ancestors, all those spirits who are dead and have gone before us into the Otherworld. There they meet with or are themselves transformed into divine beings. Samhain is a time when the doorway between our world and that of our Ancestors, human and divine, is open.

It was traditional to leave open the entrances to the great neolithic burial mounds, such as Brugh na Boinne in Ireland, at Samhain so that the spirits of the dead could come out and walk upon the earth. Sometimes at Samhain the bones of the Ancestors would be removed from the long barrows and taken to the sacred enclosures of the ancestors which were earlier built on the tops of hills for celebration, before being returned once again to the Mother's Womb.

This festival of the Ancestors continued in the Christian church's takeover of the old pagan (of the country people) festivals. On All Hallows

Eve, 31st October, the church still recognises the powers of the supernatural in their services. November 1st is All Saints Day, when the special dead - Ancestors or Goddesses and Gods now called Saints, are honoured and November 2nd is All Souls Day when all the dead are remembered.

Hallowe'en and Bonfire Night

Echoes of the ancient festival of the Death Mother still come down to us in our celebrations of Hallowe'en and Bonfire Night. Hallowe'en is a dangerous night when the veils between the worlds grow thinner and ancestors, ghosts, demons and other non-human

Beautifully carved pumpkin with the Goddess's face on a Samhain altar at the White Spring, Glastonbury

creatures may slip through the crack between the worlds and walk upon the earth. Children dress up as witches and warlocks, as the Hag Goddess, or as ancient British shamanka and shamans. Like naughty elves and fairies they go trick or treating on their neighbours.

At Hallowe'en we hollow out pumpkins shaped like the Crone's Cauldron. We carve Her face upon them and lighting them from within we show them in our windows to ward off evil. We play apple games - bobbing for apples in bowls of water and throwing apple halves to partners

across a fire. Apples are sacred to the Dark Goddess in Britain. Cutting an apple across reveals a fivefold pentacle of pips at the Core, symbol of Kore the Underworld Goddess.

Avalon – Western Isle of the Dead

Apples cut across reveal the fivefold pentacle of Kore, Kernel, Underworld Goddess at the core.

Avalon means the *place of apples* and at Glastonbury in Somerset which is the outer expression of the Isle of Avalon, apple orchards cover the slopes of the hills. The Isle of Avalon is the Otherworldly Paradise also known as the Western Isle of the Dead which is ruled by an awesome and powerful Dark Goddess of death and transformation. It was to this mysterious Isle that King Arthur was taken as he was dying, by Three or Nine Fairy Queens, Crones or Hags.

Apple orchards of Avalon in the mist

The Isle of Avalon is guarded by the Nine Morgens, the most famous of whom is Morgan La Fey or Morg-ana the Fate, the third Fate who cuts the cord of life at the moment of death. She is the Hag of the triple

Goddess Ana in whose care King Arthur is said to be sleeping until his regeneration is complete with His Queen Gwenhwyfar. For the Bringer of Death is also a Goddess of Healing and Rebirth and one aspect does not exist without the other.

Mists cover the sacred land of the Isle of Avalon, a place of mystery and magic.

It is believed by some that in earlier days this Western Isle of the Dead which was once surrounded by water, was a place for sky burial and the laying out of bodies or parts of bodies on the summit of Glastonbury Tor to be eaten by carrion birds.

Ancient Mortuary Practices

Archaeological evidence from neolithic times points to the idea that the bodies of the dead were laid out for sky burial in high places or were left in special mortuary houses until the flesh had dropped from the bones, before being placed inside a burial chamber. Indications are that bones were interred at Samhain and revisited annually. This practice is still carried out in cultures which revere their ancestors, such as the people of Madagascar. The skeletons were often curled in a foetal position as they returned to the Mother's Womb/Tomb.

Crone Goddess

The bonfire lit on November 5th was originally a *bone* fire, when flesh was burned off the bones of the dead. Whole skeletons and more often, selected bones and skulls of celebrated ancestors were placed within the ancient burial mounds to await regeneration of the whole person.

Shamanic Initiations

Crystals fill the bones of the shaman by Willow Roe

In male shamanic rituals of initiation from Siberia to Australia to North America, there is an almost universal theme of symbolic death and regeneration in the Cave, Womb or Cauldron of the Death Mother. In trance and dreams the candidate for initiation experiences his bones being stripped of flesh, often by his shaman ancestors and then chopped up into pieces, the flesh being burned on a fire. In visions the shaman sees selected bones such as the skull, shoulder, thigh or shin bone being filled with crystals, pebbles and energies which give the shaman new talents on his return to everyday life.

The selected partial remains of skeletons which are found in many burial mounds represent the vital bones which contain the gifts to be found in the spirit world. They also implied the potential to regenerate a whole person from one or two bones. It suggests that the barrows were placed of initiation rituals for shamans, who could heal and guide the whole tribe. Women shamankas were Soul Midwives guiding the dead to the shores of the Otherworld.

Guy Fawkes

Each November 5th in England we burn effigies of Guy Fawkes, who once plotted to blow up the British Houses of Parliament. The potency which still surrounds the ritual burning of this figure comes from a much earlier memory of the annual sacrifice of the Year King, who was the Goddess's human consort. It was his death and regeneration in the form of a newly Chosen One, who would then reign with the Goddess for a few days, a week or a year, which was believed to ensure the fertility of the land.

Renewal of the Clans

At Samhain the rites of renewal of the clans were also enacted, the Totem spirits of the different tribes being invoked and revered. The shamanka and shaman would wear their swan, owl and eagle feathers, their bear, boar, wolf, or cat skins. They danced their totems into life. The dead who had returned to their Primal originating Ancestors were honoured.

In Keltic legend Swan Maidens, Swan Princesses and Swan Princes who had lived for a time as humans had to resume their birdlike forms at Samhain. In the Dream of Oengus mac Oc, Oengus dreams of a beautiful Swan coming out of a lake onto the shore and removing her feathers. She transforms into a beautiful Maiden whose name is Caer (or Ker), with whom he instantly falls in love. At Samhain she resumes her true form as a beautiful white swan. In order to be with her, Oengus agrees to be himself transformed into a swan. Together the two white swans circles the lake three times singing the Noble Strain which lulls all listeners to sleep.

The Shamanaka dons her swan feathers to dance her totem into life.

Talismans of the Death Mother

The Death Mother has two main talismans. The first is the Moon Sickle or Scissors with which She cuts the grain as part of the grain cycle. As the third of the three Fates the Sickle is also used to cut the thread of life at the moment of death. The Scissors appear in early legend with Rhiannon's Comb as prizes sought by heroes from between the ears of the deadly Wild Boar which once roamed the ancient forests. To capture these talismans was to be magically protected from death.

Her second talisman is the Cauldron of Death and Regeneration into which all souls are plunged when Her scissors have cut the cords of life. See Keridwen later.

The Hag Goddess

The Hag begins Her reign at Samhain when She takes back the white rod of power from Brigit, who has held it since Imbolc throughout the spring and summer. The white rod is transformed by Her touch into the black rod of winter and the Hag blasts the land with cold and darkness, withering all the vegetation. In the initiatory cycle of the year the Hag is Guardian of the gateway to the dark, hibernatory part of the year. She is the Bringer of Death. The warmth of summer is over and at Her touch all nature slows. The sap begins to retreat into the roots of plants and trees and leaves turn golden, orange, red and brown and blown by the autumn gales fall from the trees. Animals prepare to go into hibernation when they will sleep through the cold winter months, living on stored fats and slowing their breathing and heart rates.

The Corn Hag

In Scotland it was the custom until recent times for the last sheaf of corn harvested to be fashioned into the likeness of a woman with dock and ragweed stalks, and tied with coloured threads. In Argyllshire, Perth, Uist and other places She was called the Corn Hag or the Famine of the Farm. The man who cut the last sheaf was called Winter and dirty water was thrown at him, his face was blackened and he was rolled up in canvas.

It was believed that death would come to the man and his stock who held the Corn Hag, so no-one wanted to have Her to support all winter. When a man had finished cutting his own corn he sent his Corn Hag to a man who had not yet finished harvesting. This was considered unlucky and a great insult to the recipients, sometimes resulting in bloodshed. The Hag had to be conveyed cautiously. A young man on a horse would gallop at full speed as if on urgent business, past his neighbour's uncut field. He then would throw the Corn Hag into the field and gallop away.

However a man who did this on South Uist was pursued and brought back. His pursuers shaved his beard off and made a "clipping of bird and of fool (bird droppings)" on him and sent him home. Another was stripped, dipped and sent home naked. A crofter would rather see his best cow dead than see the Corn Hag on his harvest rig. (*Ortho Nangaidheal* by Alexander Carmichael).

To the present day in Scotland the Lammas Corn Dolly becomes the Corn Hag as She dries out and withers. In Britain the Corn Hag was called Harvest May, Harvest Bride or Ivy Girl after the ivy which was used to blind the sheaf or corn. Like the Corn Hag She was considered an ill omen for the farmer who was last to bring his harvest home.

Cale, Kali

Scotland was once known as Caledonia, the land given by Cale or Kali, who is the Samhain version of Ker. At Callanish on the Isle of Lewis a beautiful group of standing stones are aligned to the cycles of the sun and moon. Callanish or Callernish has been translated as Cale's headland, while its Gaelic name of Tursachan, means place of mourning (for the dead) or place of pilgrimage (to the ancestors). (*New Light on the Stones of Callanish* by Margaret and Gerald Ponting).

Above: The stones of Callanish on the Isle of Lewis in Scotland are aligned to the movements of the sun and moon.
Below: the face of Black Kali, the destroyer of evil force

Cale is related to Kali as Destroyer. Like Kali She was said to be a black or blue Giantess who founded many races of people and created the world, building mountain ranges from the stones that dropped from Her apron. The stones of several burial chambers in Wales and Scotland are said to have fallen from the Goddess's apron. Barclodiad Y Garvres is a dolmen on Anglesey, known as the Giantess's Apronful. There are others.

In the Indian *Devi-Mahatmaya* written c.400 CE, Black Kali was said to have sprung forth from the brow of the Great Goddess Durga during Her battle with the demonic asuras. With a great roar and wielding knives and weapons She is an awe-inspiring Destroyers of evil force.

Crone Goddess

Willow pointed out that the description of Black Kali as an emanation of Durga, is identical to that of the Goddess of the Picts in Scotland, who is also described as being blue-back and a frightening wielder of knives.

In an interesting sidelight St. George, the English Dragon Slayer was said to be the son of Mother Caleb, another version of Cale, Kali, Ker.

Scota

The young Maiden pricks Her finger on the sharp spindle of the Dark Fairy's Spinning Wheel signalling her initiation into womanhood. Drawing by Willow Roe.

The name for Scotland is derived from Scota or Scotia, the Goddess known as the Dark One, who was equated with Bera, the Hag of Winter. To the Kelts She was known as the Warrior Queen Skathac who lived on the Isle of Skye. To the Scandinavians who had a later influence on Scotland She was Skadi or Skuld. Skuld was the Destroying Crone, the third of the three Norns or Fates, who sat at the Well of Urd in roots of the World Tree Yggdrasil, spinning the Web of Fate.

The Old Hag in Folklore

There are many folk tales in which an Old Hag or Dark or Thirteenth Fairy plays an important role, often leading the hera or hero to their death or into a deep transforming sleep, behind the high walls of a castle surrounded by an impenetrable forest, or within a glass coffin or on the Isle of Glass.

Sleeping Beauty pricks her finger on the spindle of Fate of the Dark Fairy's spinning wheel and falls into a deep sleep which lasts for a hundred years. She and all her courtiers lie undisturbed until she is awakened by the kiss of a prince. Snow White takes a bite from the Old Crone's apple of transformation and falls into a deathlike sleep, again to be awakened by a kiss from the prince. The prick of the spindle of Fate and the bite of the Dark Goddess's apple initiates the process of transformation from childhood to womanly sexual awakening.

Crone Goddess

Merlin was said to have been entrapped by Nimue, the Hag disguised as beautiful Maiden, on a Glass Island, where he guards the Thirteen Treasures of Britain and awaits rebirth. These stories symbolise rites of passage of the Hag Goddess, riddles to be solved on the road to transformation.

Chivalrous Knight Gawain meets the Ugly Dame Ragnall. Drawing by Willow Roe

In Arthurian legend King Arthur is challenged by a giant, Gromer Somer Joure, to discover what it is that women desire. Arthur asks his champion knight, Gawain to help solve the riddle. Out riding one day they meet an ugly Old Hag, Dame Ragnell, who says She will tell them the answer to the riddle if Gawain marries Her. Chivalrous knight that he is Gawain agrees to marry the hideous wart-covered Old Woman. On their wedding night the ugly old Dame asks Gawain for a kiss, which our hero is fortunately able to give. Immediately the Hag is transformed into a beautiful woman.

Crone Goddess

But She can only be beautiful for half the day. She tells Gawain that he must choose whether he wishes Her to be fair by day and ugly by night or ugly by day and fair by night. Unable to choose he asks Her to decide for Herself. And that is the solution to the riddle - what women want is to be able to choose for ourselves. Gawain tell Arthur the solution to the riddle and he tells it to the Giant, who exclaims that only His sister (the Giantess/Goddess) could have given them the right answer. Unfortunately for Arthur and the women of his era, the King did not heed this solution in his own life. When Gwenhwyfar tries to lead Her own life loving whom She chooses She is branded as the Arthur's betrayer and cast out from his court

The Grand Mothers

'Crowning the Crones' ceremony at the 1999 Goddess Conference honoured the Grand Mothers in our community. Singer Julie Felix is centre right.

Hidden within the depths of many legends and folk tales is a memory of a time when the Old Woman was honoured. She now appears as the Wicked Step-Mother, the Wicked Witch and the ugly old Crone, all inversions of an earlier honouring of the Wise Old Woman. In many indigenous traditions the Grandmothers are the Keepers of the wisdom of the tribe. In Native American tradition each of the original thirteen Clans is represented by a Granmother Medicine Bundle which contains

the most important medicine or teachings of the clan. Once upon a time each of these Grandmother Bundles had its own Lodge or Tipi, which was guarded by the Warriors of the tribe. Only the Grandmothers, the wise women elders, were permitted to enter the lodge.

There are hints of a similar honouring of the Old Woman and the Grandmothers amongst our earliest ancestors. It can be seen in the inversion of awe for the Death Goddess into fear of and disrespect to the Hag and in the derogatory names given to older women.

The Grandmothers are those who after the menopause retain Her blood within their wombs and thus becomes wise. We have almost completely lost their experience and wisdom in our society. As I get older and enjoy the maturity of my older women friends and grand mothers, I would love to see that proper honouring of the older woman come back.

Honour to the Grandmothers!
Honour to the Old Women!

Crone Goddess

Sheela-Na-Gig

Sheela na Gig

Sheela-na-Gig is the squatting Hag, whose hands hold open Her yawning Gig Vulva. Hers is the most blatantly sexual image to be found in the pantheon of early British Goddesses and Gods. Carvings of Her are to be seen in churches all over Brigit's Isles, particularly in Ireland and Wales, where Her image was used as a gargoyle to frighten away demons. One of the most widely illustrated is to be found in the church of St. Mary and St. David's at Kilpeck in Herefordshire. There is a lovely one on the outside of the Nunnery on the Isle of Iona. In churches dedicated to St. Brigit, Sheela-na-Gig is often seen carved over the porch. To enter the church through the arched doorway was to symbolically pass through the Yoni of the Goddess.

Sheela na Gig carved on the outside of St Mary and St David's church at Kilpeck in Herefordshire

The locations of 150 Sheela na Gigs are listed in a wonderful book *The Sheela-na-Gigs of Ireland and Britain* by Joanne McMahon and Jack Roberts.

The Bird Goddess

Sheela-na-Gig has several interesting features. The first is Her Hag's head which is usually ugly and often triangular-shaped, with a broad brow, protruding eyes and a small pointed chin. This shape is found in early carvings from Old Europe of the Bird and Snake Goddess (*Goddesses and Gods of Old Europe* by Marija Gimbutas). It is also

seen in representations of early Ancestors and of insect-like extraterrestrial beings. Sheela's breasts are usually withered or not visible and She is often shown with the protruding ribcage of an Old Woman.

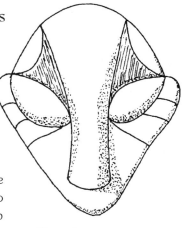

Her Sacred Yoni

Sheela's most prominent feature is Her gaping Yoni, the place where Her power lies. The Yoni of the Hag Mother is the gateway to death and a return to Her Womb of Regeneration. It is to this Womb that all souls are returned at the end of earthly life to await rebirth. Unlike the worships of later Gods who glorified the head and out of body experiences, the worship of the early Goddess lay in the body. In particular She was to be experienced in the surrender or little death of sexual communion between women and men. Women who identified with the Goddess gave of Her *karuna* or sexual love. Men made love to the Goddess in women.

To make love is literally to generate the energy of love, which is powerful and transformative. It is one of the secrets of the sacred Yoni, that women know instinctually when we make love and which increases as we mature. In our society we pay lip service to the power of sex by denigrating and exploiting women's and men's bodies and sexuality for material gain. Its spiritual power is denied and feared since it leads to loss of personality control and the necessary death of the ego.

This Ancestral head from the Vinca culture, Yugoslavia, 4,500 BCE, has a similar shape to that of many Sheela na Gigs.

Opposite: Sheela na Gig carving above the window on the outside wall of the Nunnery on the island of Iona.

Vesica Piscis

Sheela's Gig Vulva is shaped like a mandorla, the yonic shape created from the two interlocking circles of the Vesica Pisces symbol. In ancient times this vesica piscis (vessel of the fish) shape universally symbolised the Yoni of the Goddess long before it was taken over by Christian artists as representing the Piscean Age. The vesica piscis appears in many religious paintings, stained glass windows and church archways. It is the foundation pattern for the sacred geometry used to build cathedrals. It is often a container for the image of Jesus. What was forgotten was that Jesus the Son was always contained by the Vulva of the Great Mother.

Vesica Piscis

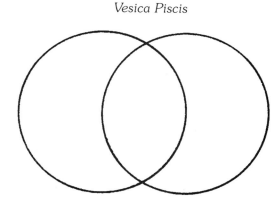

Kali

The worship of the Goddess as the Great Yoni is one of the earliest and most universal beliefs found throughout the world. It is still found today in the worship of Kali and Shakti in India. Many statues of Kali in Hindu temples show an open and gaping Vulva and worshippers will lick a finger and touch Her Yoni for luck. The oldest statues have deep holes worn away by thousands of years of veneration.

A famous temple at Kamakhya in Assam is dedicated to the worship of the Goddess's Yoni. It was said that Shiva became inconsolable when his beloved wife Sati died. He wandered the earth in a mad dance with Sati's dead body on his shoulder. Vishnu who was following Shiva to make sure he was alright, cut up Sati's body piece by piece to relieve Shiva's burden. Where fragments of Her body fell,

Adoration of the the Sacred Yoni at the Sixty Four Yogini Temple, Madhya Pradesh, Assam, India. drawing by Diana Griffiths

fifty one Shakti-pithas or pilgrimage centres came into being. Sati's Vulva fell at Kamakhya and a temple was built on the hilltop to mark the spot.

Here there is no image of the Goddess but in the depths of the shrine is a yoni-shaped cleft in the rock adored as the Yoni of Shakti. A natural spring within the cave keeps the cleft moist. During July and August after the first burst of the monsoon a great ceremony takes place when the water runs red with iron oxide. This ritual drink is drunk as the menstrual blood of the Goddess and is believed to be sacred and an object of veneration. *(Kali, the Feminine Force* by Ajit Mookerjee).

Initiation Through Her Yoni

A return to the Womb of the Mother through Her Yoni is the basis of nearly all forms of initiatory rites in so-called primitive societies. These rites usually involve bodily decoration, often with red pigments symbolising the blood of the womb, and then entrance to an enclosed womb-like space through a narrow passageway. Here the candidate for initiation remains for up to three days - the length of time in each lunar month that the Moon remains hidden from view. The Moon God is beneath the earth making love to the Sun Goddess. At the end of this time the initiate emerges symbolically reborn from the Vulva of the Goddess.

In the western world worship of the Yoni has all but been stamped out by rigid Christian and Muslim orthodoxies, which have viewed sex and women as temptations of the Devil to be avoided at all cost. The unconscious distorted veneration of the Yoni is however visible in the vast amount of pornography which displays and denigrates the sacred Yoni of women. At the time of writing 30% of all Internet websites are pornographic in nature. We can still find traces of the earlier worship of Her Sacred Yoni in the placing of Sheela-na-Gig in churches and the thread of worship of Mary Magdalene, the Sacred Harlot, that still exists in Britain, France and some parts of Europe.

Mary Magdalene

Mary Magdalene, the Redeemed Whore of Christianity, was named in Irish writing as a *kelle* or priestess of the Goddess Kelle. The Keltic Kele or Kale was the same Goddess as the Indian Kali. Mary Magdalene represents the Dark unacceptable face of the Triple Mary Goddess. She is the Sacred Whore who invites all to share the Mother's sexual love. She is the Black Goddess who like Kali created the world through Her

Mary Magdalene, the Redeemed Whore of Christianity often appears as the Death Goddess with a skull at Her feet.

Willow Roe

171

Crone Goddess

Vulva. It is Mary Magdalene as the Death Goddess who anoints the soon to be sacrificed king with oil. In paintings and sculptures Mary Magdalene often appears as the Death Goddess, with a skull at Her feet.

Natural Clefts

The worship of the Vulva and Womb of the Earth Mother has existed from the beginning of human life on earth. In many places throughout the world natural rock formations are regarded as openings into Her sacred Body and honoured as such. Caves too are regarded as openings into Her Womb. Pilgrims who crawl through a rocky underground tunnel representing the birth canal, are regarded as born again from the Yoni of the Goddess.

Natural cleft in the rock wall at Ebbor Gorge, Somerset, which looks like the Goddess's Vulva

Dolmens and Passage Graves

In Britain and abroad the earliest megalithic mounds, passage graves and dolmens - three or more standing stones with a capstone, were built to represent the Death Goddess's Vulva and Womb/Tomb of Regeneration. Their entrances are shaped to resemble to Great Mother's Yonic gateway and inside a narrow vaginal passageway opens out into a wider womb space. The passages may be short or long, straight or angled just like a woman's vagina and cervix. Some ritual mounds are entered by squeezing between closely positioned Yonic stones and some passage graves can be entered only through a small round porthole.

The Yonic gateway of Men-an-tol in Cornwall. Once covered by a mound of earth the central chamber could only be entered by squeezing through the holed stone. Today those wishing to be healed must squeeze through the holed stone three times back and forth.

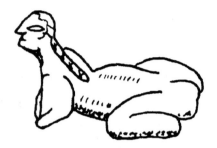

Image of Frog with a Vulva on her back by Diana Griffiths

Goddess as Toad from Hacilar, Anatolia, 5000BCE by KJ

Crone Goddess

The Frog Goddess of Death and Regeneration

The derivation of the word Sheela-na-Gig is obscure but probably means the Old Woman with Vulva. According to Marija Gimbutas in *The Language of the Goddess*, this image is derived from the early Frog Goddess. Images of the Frog or Toad Goddess with outstretched bent limbs and a human vulva are found dating from the earliest times. They are carved in stone and clay, excised and engraved on stone and ceramics. Often they combine a woman's head with the body of a frog.

In folklore the frog and toad have long been associated with the Goddess of Death and Regeneration. As a messenger of death a Toad may crawl onto the chest of a sleeping person and suck the breath from their body, causing certain death. An angry toad is said to puff herself up until she explodes, releasing a virulent poison which can kill. Toads are the familiars of witches and of Hecate, the Underworld Goddess who in Greek legend was known as Baubo, meaning toad. In British legend one of the Oldest Creatures in the World is the Toad of Cors Vochno.

Keridwen The Underworld Goddess

Keridwen is the Underworld Goddess, the great White Sow into whose Cauldron all souls will return for regeneration and inspiration. She is a Shape Shifter and Underworld Initiator. Encounters with Keridwen are powerful and transformative. She has similar qualities to the Underworld Goddesses of other cultures, such as Ereshkigal in the Sumerian myths; the Teutonic Freya who is called Syr or Sow; and to Demeter as Destroyer, who was known as Phorcis the Sow. Her impact cannot be avoided or turned aside. One of the most revered Dakinis in Tantric Buddhism is Vajravarahi, the Diamond Sow.

Wild pigs both as Sow and Boar have long been associated with death. They are scavengers who like vultures eat corpses. There are paintings of boars alongside bison in caves at Altamira in Spain from the Magdalenian Epoch of 12,000 BCE. In Irish myth the Boar was a beast of death. It was one of his poisonous bristles which killed Diarmuid, the lover of Grainne, the Sun Goddess, In several legends through the ages different parts of Britain were ravaged by wild boars, with dangerous poisonous bristles. The boar was believed to have magical properties including a comb and scissors between its ears, which had to be seized by pursing heroes.

In a shrine dating from c.6,000BCE at Çatal Huyuk in Turkey, large female breasts cover the lower jaws and tusks of enormous boars. In a shrine next to this, breasts cover vulture skulls. Life encloses and triumphs over death. In Britain the lower jaw of boars have been found buried in front of Hetty Pegler's Tump, a megalithic tomb in the Cotswolds, and at Hanging Grimstone in Yorkshire dating from 3540 BCE. (*The Language of the Goddess* by Marija Gimbutas).

The Sow is the sacred animal of the Pregnant Death Goddess. She is pregnant both with life and with the souls of the dead. In Europe there are many sculptures and vases of Sows dating from the 7th to 3rd millennium BCE. There are statuettes and paintings of Sow masked dancers in early Greek shrines. The Sow was sacred to the Grain Goddess as Demeter and Ker.

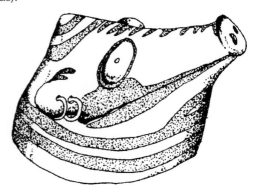

Sow Goddess vase from S. Romania c. 4520BCE by Diana Griffiths

Suckling pigs were among the main offerings to Demeter and Her daughter Persephone in the Greek autumn sowing festival of Thesmophoria. This rite was performed solely by women for three days in October like our own Samhain. Women brought the remains of suckling pigs which had been left to rot for three months in underground caves. The remains were placed on altars with pine cones and wheat cakes in the shape of male genitals. They were then all mixed with the seeds which were to be used for sowing. The decomposed flesh of the pig increased the fertility of the seeds. (*The Language of the Goddess* by Marija Gimbutas).

The Sow and Boar are Totem Ancestors for the early British people. Their direction on Britannia's Sacred Wheel lies in the northwest. Their festival and rites of renewal take place at Samhain. Many British people still have a prohibition against the eating of pig flesh, the sign of an earlier totem taboo.

Throughout Europe the Sow Goddess is the double of the Grain Goddess, Ker or Demeter. In Britain there is little remaining archeological

Crone Goddess

evidence for the worship of the Sow Goddess and our information is derived from mythological and intuitive sources. Keridwen is our Underworld Sow Goddess. The most well known story about Her is told in the Welsh Romance of Taliesin and again I shall retell this tale in my own fashion.

The Inspiration of Taliesin

Keridwen lived on an island in the middle of Lake Tegid (Lake Bala in North Wales), which She ruled as Lady of the Lake. She had two children, Creirwy or Ker-eirwy, the most beautiful girl in the world and Afagddu the ugliest boy. To compensate for Afagddu's ugliness Keridwen decided in due time to gift him with inspiration and knowledge from Her Cauldron of Wisdom.

Her Cauldron was to be found in the Otherworld where it had to simmer for a year and a day before it was ready to drink. Magical herbs and flowers were added with the passing of each season, gathered at their appropriate astrological hour. An Old Man was given the task of stirring the pot while a Young Boy, Gwion had to fetch wood each day for the fire.

One day towards the end of the year as the Cauldron was being stirred three burning drops flew out of it and fell on Gwion's finger. He put it in his mouth to cool the burn and at once understood the nature and meaning of all things past, present and future. Gwion fled from his new-found knowledge.

Keridwen knew instantly what had happened and changing Herself into a screaming black Hag chased after the fleeing Gwion. The three drops of the magical brew also allowed Gwion to change his shape. Keridwen of course was a shapeshifter Herself and the two began to shapeshift through the Totem creatures of the Welsh Medicine Wheel.

Gwion first changed himself into a hare but Keridwen changed into a greyhound and pursued him. Gwion plunged into a river to become a fish and Keridwen became the faster swimming otter. He flew into the air as a bird but Keridwen became the hunting hawk. Gwion changed himself into a single grain in a pile of wheat on the floor of a barn and Keridwen transformed herself into a black crested hen. She scratched through the grain with Her feet and found Gwion and ate him up.

When She came back to Herself, Virgin Goddess that She is, Keridwen found herself pregnant. Nine months later She gave birth to a

Crone Goddess

Willow Roe

beautiful boy and Gwion's ugliness had been transformed. Keridwen no longer had the heart to kill him and tying him in a leather bag - always a symbol for Her Womb, She threw him into the sea two days before Mayday.

The boy in the bag was carried to a weir in Cardigan Bay where he was rescued by a certain Prince Elphin (from *Elph, Aelph* meaning *Shining One* of the Tuatha de Danaan), who had come there to fish. Prince Elphin was pleased with his catch and renamed the little Gwion, Taliesin, meaning *fine value* and *beautiful brow*.

Taliesin went on to become known as an inspired poet and seer. He was particularly famous for his riddles, which when spoken and solved could change the weather and break the strongest chains. As a child Taliesin rescued his own rescuer Elphin from imprisonment by reciting this riddle before his captor:

> *Discover what it is*
> *The strong creature from before the Flood*
> *Without flesh, without bone*
> *Without vein, without blood,*

Without hands, without feet...
In field, in forest...
Without hand, without foot.
It is also as wide
As the surface of the earth,
And it was not born,
Nor was it seen.

Following pages:
Overleaf: The Keres or
Fates are death-
dealing Bird Women,
descendants of the
Vulture Goddess by
Thalia Brown
Colour: Detail of Toad
at the Oracle of
Nights. Painting by
Carolyn Hillyer

The solution to the riddle came as a violent wind which frightened Elphin's captor into bringing Elphin up from his dungeon. Taliesin unchained him by reciting an incantation. (From *The White Goddess* by Robert Graves)

Keridwen the Fate

In Taliesin's story of death and regeneration from Keridwen's Cauldron, we see Keridwen as the third of the three Fates, the Goddess of Death and the Pregnant Goddess of Rebirth. It is by accident, by Fate, that Gwion is splashed by the magical three drops from Her Cauldron. It is only then when he wishes to run away from His Fate taking his new found knowledge with him, that Keridwen pursues and consumes him as the Death Goddess.

As the Goddess of Fate who eats up souls Keridwen is associated with the Keres or Fates of Death of Greek myth, who are portrayed as death-dealing Black Bird women or Black Hens. Descended from the ancient Vulture Goddess (or other Bird of Prey Goddess) they are portrayed as having women's heads and vulture's feet. The maligned Bird Goddess Lilith is one well-known example. In Ireland She was known as the Morrigan who flew over the battlefields calling in the souls of dead soldiers. The Keres were also sometimes said to be Death Hounds - Dog-faced Furies who waited at battlefields to sweep the souls of the dead to glory. In Britain they are the red-eared White Hounds of Annwn.

The Cauldron of Rebirth

It is after being consumed by the Death Goddess that Gwion enters upon his true transformation and regeneration within the Womb bag of the Goddess. He is reborn beautiful, inspired and talented. In this myth of the transformation of the Young Boy, Gwion, the scarcely-mentioned

179

Crone Goddess

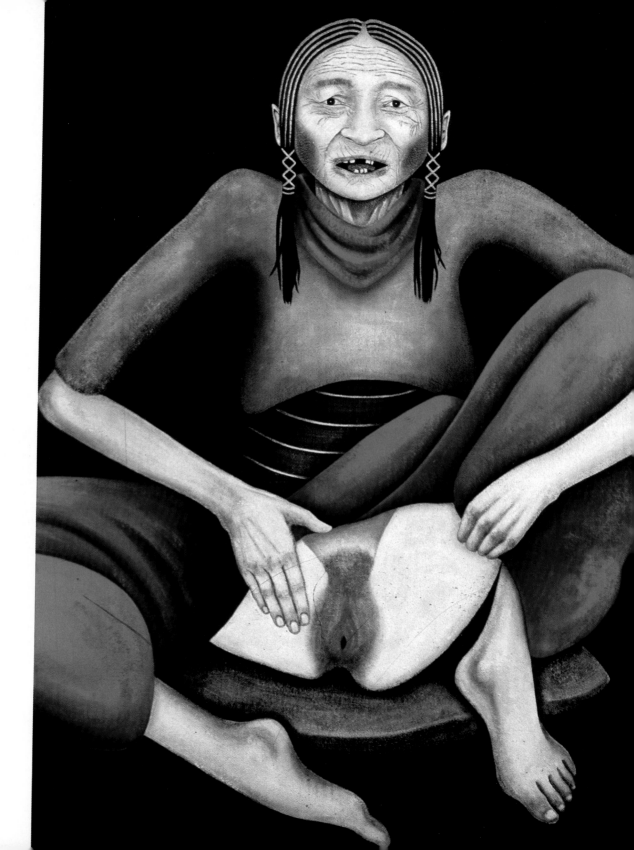

Old Man who daily stirs Keridwen's Cauldron and the rebirth of Taliesin, we have another example of an initiation rite for men. This time regeneration is completed through service to the Cauldron of the Underworld Goddess.

Images on the silver Gundestrop Cauldron show a row of candidates for initiation approaching Her Cauldron which is shield-shaped and double-lobed. A figure stands beside the Cauldron plunging the candidates in headfirst. They emerge above the Cauldron riding on horses - symbols of personal energy and power, towards the sun or even the Sun Goddess. There are many other legends and myths of people being plunged into Her Cauldron to later emerge reborn, but it is Keridwen's story that best describes the important details of the regeneration myth.

From the earliest times the Cauldron has been a magical symbol for the Crone Goddess and it has several roles and functions. It can be a Cauldron of Healing and Plenty, always full of whatever is needed. It is the Boiling Cauldron of Death and Rebirth, as well as being a Cauldron of Poetry and Inspiration.

It is in Her Cauldron that through time the Hag brews Her alchemical mixture of magical herbs, which give the ability to change shape, to travel between the worlds, to know the past, present and future. Once Her three drops have been touched there is no turning back from the Underworld transformation that feels like death and lasts for at least nine months. It is a long process, suspended in Her amniotic Life-giving fluid, but the initiate emerges reborn, imbued with Her life, inspiration, poetry and beauty.

Opposite above: Self-initiated Priest/esses of Avalon 2001
Below: Banner of the Nine Morgens at the Goddess Conference main altar, painted by Thalia Brown.

Willow Roe

Keridwen's Cauldron of Poetry, Inspiration and Regeneration

Mother of Air
Danu, Aine, Arianrhod

Opposite:modern day stone sculpture of the Omphalos of Anu in front of the Paps.

The Paps of Anu, County Kerry in Ireland

The Mother of Air in the North is Danu, Anu, Aine, Arianrhod, Mother of the limitless Sky and Goddess of the Tuatha de Danaan, who built the stone circles in the late neolithic era. As Danu She is remembered throughout Brigit's Isles but particularly in Ireland where She is described by Cormac as the Mother of all the Irish gods and a sister to Grian the

Opposite: "The White Death Goddess with Her Dog at Dawn" Painting by Foosiya Miller

Sun Goddess. As Aine the meanings of Her name include delight, joy, harmony, pleasure, brightness, brilliance, splendour, and glory.

As Mother of Air She lives beyond the North Wind, and is Goddess of the Hyperboreans. She is the stillness at the centre of a storm, the stillness that comes after death when the turbulence of life has passed away. Hers is the energy of the Bardo state of consciousness which lies between death and rebirth. She is Stone Woman, Bird Woman, Bone Woman. She is the Cailleach of Winter and the Death. Goddess.

Cailleach of Winter

The Cailleach or in Irish the Caillighe, is the Old Woman or Hag of Winter. In the cycle of the seasons She begins Her reign at Samhain when She takes back the white rod of power from Brigit, who has held it throughout the spring and summer. The white rod is transformed by Her touch into the icy black rod of winter and the Cailleach soon blasts the land with cold and darkness. She governs the winter moons from Samhain to Imbolc and Her qualities are celebrated at the Winter Solstice.

The Cailleach touches the grass with frost and ice.

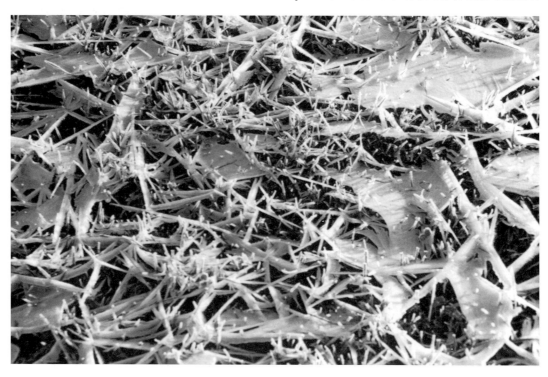

The body of the Sleeping Woman covered in winter snow in Avalon

In the initiatory cycle of the year in Brigit's Isles the Cailleach rules the dark, hibernatory part of the year. She is the Grain Goddess in mourning for the loss of Her daughter the Maiden Kernel, who has descended into the Underworld to be with Her Grandmother Keridwen. All of Her nature sleeps. Human beings naturally turn inwards, reaching into the dark recesses of our souls, sitting in stillness or absorbed by television. Like the chrysalis that hangs motionless on the tree until spring, all life is suspended by the touch of the Cailleach's icy rod.

In Irish tradition the Cailleach or Caillighe is the aged goddess who is the primal eternal Mother of the province of Ulster. She is regarded as the impersonator of winter and the harbinger of spring. She lives in the north and is infinitely old but still has many lovers. There is a story in which She entices the solar hero, Finn McCool, into Her house - a stone burial chamber,

> *"He went in fresh and youthful, and came out a done old man.......a wedding party went into Caille Berry's House (Cailleach Bheare's house) and they were turned into stone."*
>
> *Mythic Ireland* by Michael Dames

Cailleach Bheare

The Cailleach Bheare or Hag of Bheare lives on the Bheare peninsula in County Kerry in the southwest of Ireland. There She is remembered as the Shaper of the Land, the Builder of the Mountains which form the backbone of the peninsula. Cailleach Bheare is regarded as the mother of the Goddess Aine. She is one of three primal Goddesses associated with the three peninsulas of County Kerry - the other two being Cailleach Bholais, Goddess of the Ring of Kerry, and Cailleach Daingin being Goddess of the Dingle peninsula. The name Bheare is derived from the same root as the Cow Goddess Bo, Boi or Boand, who later became Brigit.

In the mythology of the region it is believed that the great Cailleach is now transformed into a small rocky outcrop overlooking the sea at Coulagh Bay on the northwestern side of the Bheare peninsula. Far away and hard to get to, a small well-worn path leads from the road to a curious outcrop of rock signposted as the Hag of Bheare.

The Cailleach Bheare is obviously honoured to the present day as the rock is covered in small stones and other offerings - a small goddess included, which are arranged in every nook and cranny. The rock itself is a geological oddity, being of a lump of metamorphic rock, which is the only one of its kind found within the whole southwestern region, a reminder of the Goddess as the Shaper of the Land. She is said to be waiting for Her lover, the Sea God Manannan Mac Lir to return to Her from the sea.

The whole rock can be seen as the Cailleach Bheare's head or Her profile can been seen in the left edge of the rock.

Cailleach na Montaigne

Some mountains in Scotland are named after the Cailleach where She was known as Cailleach na Montaigne - the Old Woman of the Mountains. She was called Carline and Mag-Moullach and Bera, who lived on the mountain top of Ben Nevis. It was here that She was said to hold Brigit prisoner through the winter months, Her silver hammer turning the world to ice.

Cailleach na Mointeach

The Pairc Mountains which form the horizon to the southeast of the Callanish stones show the profile of a sleeping woman, sometimes called the Sleeping Beauty. In Gaelic She is known as Cailleach na Mointeach - the Old Woman of the Moors. It is between these mountains that the moon skims the horizon during the extreme southern moonrise revery 18.67 years as viewed from the Callanish stones, connecting Brigit who rules the sun/moon cycle to the Cailleach.

As the Sleeping Woman of Winter She is the Great Sleeper Dreamer in whose Dreaming Womb our universe is created. She dreams our world alive as She lies sleeping.

Arianrhod of the Silver Wheel

Arianrhod of the Silver Wheel is a leading character in the Welsh *Romance of Math ap Mathonwy*. Arianrhod is the "Silver Circled daughter of Don" or in Her original form, the "Silver Circled daughter of Danu". She is a daughter and herself a Mother Goddess.

In the Romance Arianrhod is called to be a Footholder to Math ap Mathonwy. As She enters his court he decides to test whether or not She is still a Virgin and asks Her to step over his magic wand. As She does so She gives birth to boy twins, one of whom is Dylan of the Wave, who like Jesus, is a divine Fish Child. The second twin is fostered with the magician Gwydion. After killing a Wren on Old Christmas day he becomes the Sun Hero, LLew LLaw Gyffes - the Lion with a Steady Hand. In the Romance Arianrhod is apparently tricked into giving Her son his name and a set of fighting arms, indicating that Her story comes

Opposite: Painting of Arianrhod by Jane Brideson

188

arianrhod

from early matriarchal times when all power was vested in the Goddess and She was recognised as such. Later in the story Arianrhod adopts the form of the Love Goddess Blodeuwedd and through various treacheries destroys Her grown son Llew Llaw Gyffes. Blodeuwedd herself is transformed first into the Owl of Wisdom and then into Keridwen, the Old Sow who eats Her offspring, who eats up Llew's flesh. Llew's soul takes the form of an eagle which flies up into the sky and is later restored to life. The full complex story is retold in Robert Graves' wonderful *White Goddess*. It was the foundation myth for *The Sacred Marriage* a play which I wrote for Ariadne Productions, which was performed in 1993 (See *On Finding Treasure*).

Arianrhod is a transforming Goddess who brings Death in Life and Life in Death. She lives far beyond the North Wind in the Land of the Dead in Her Castle of Caer Arianrhod, which is equated with the constellation of Corona Borealis, the Crown of the North Wind. Corona Borealis is also called the Kretan Crown, Corona Ariadnae and is sacred to the Kretan Goddess Ariadne.

Ariadne is the High Fruitful Mother of the Barley , the Very Holy, Very Manifest One, the Wise Virgin, Lady of the First Light, Queen of the Sun and Moon. She is Guardian of the gateways to the sevenfold Labrynth in which we journey inwards to the centre of our souls, where we face our own darkness and light and connect with the stars from which we are created. Ariadne/Arianrhod is Queen of the Dark and of the Light in the Darkness. She is the Dark Light who rules the endings of time and one of Her many names is She who closes the door to the Aeon.

Ariadne's seven circuit Labrynth

Talismans, Colours, Creatures of the North

The Cailleach's talismans are those of the Air, the element of our spiritual nature. They are the Sceptre of Sovereignty, the Sword of Light and the Feather Fan. The Sceptre is a royal symbol of our commitment to love and serve the Goddess. The Sword of Light rather than of death represents our ability to cut through to truth and reality with our vision. The Feather Fan represents our ability to fly.

As Mother of the Air Her companions are the Eagle, Buzzard, White Owl and Hawk and all the Winged Ones, including the Wren, the King of the Birds, who is traditionally honoured at Winter Solstice. As Birdwoman She offers us the gift of flight, of flying in our dreams and in our imagination to Otherworlds, journeying on Her wings into other Realms. She shows us how to live lightly on the earth and to lift out of our physical bodies on the wings of Her Spirit.

The Cailleach's festival comes at Winter Solstice, when daylight hours in the northern hemisphere are soon over and darkness reigns. Her colours are those of winter - shades of violet, silver, grey and white. In the daily cycle Her energies are those of midnight when much of life is asleep, in stasis, dreaming of the past and future. Hers is the Dark of the Moon, the days when the moon's face has disappeared from view, the time when Underworld initiations take place. Her gifts are those of the wind blowing through our lives, and the stillness of the Soul while the Cauldron of Life churns. She offers us spiritual truths and wisdom.

*Birdwoman Sculpture
by Foosiya Miller*

Goddess Loving Women of Brigit's Isles

The Goddess would not be returning to western consciousness without the love and creativity of thousands of women and men who have heard Her voice and responded to Her Call. Many women in particular are opening our hearts to Her, turning away from the power over values of patriarchal society, beginning a journey of exploration into the nature of the Divine Feminine, which changes our lives.

As a world we have lost touch with Our Mother Nature and the consequences are everywhere to be seen in the pollution of Her land, sea and air, in the violence of our societies, in the famines, plagues and wars that afflict huge numbers of the world's population. The need to remember the Goddess and Her ways has become urgent if we are to bring our world back into balance. It is a long journey and we have much to learn from the past and to create anew in the present if we are to survive on this beautiful planet, which is Her Body.

Over the last twenty five years there has been an expanding interest in Goddess all over the western world. In the east She has been continuously honoured in places like India and Sri Lanka, but these are patriarchal societies where women are often disempowered and feminine values derided. Today the return of the Goddess naturally implies the honouring of women and our values, lives, intelligence, wisdom and ideals, and the empowerment of both women and men.

The quest to reconnect with the ancient Goddess is now a living spiritual path to the Goddess, honouring Her as She appears today. In the following pages we will explore that experience through the voices and artwork of women artists, performers, writers and poets who love the Goddess. Photograhs and information are also included from the fabulous annual Glastonbury Goddess Conference, to which Goddess-

Opposite: Some of the wonderful Goddess figures created for the Glastonbury Goddess Conference over the years.
Top left: 1997 Lammas Mother Goddess made by Lucy Lepchani
Top right: Crone Goddess 1999 created by Foosiya Miller and Jackie Yeomans
Lower left: Dancing Virgin Goddess 2001 made by Foosiya Miller, Diana Milstein and friends
Lower right: Black Mother Bird Goddess 1998 made by Lucy Lepchani

192

loving women and men come from all over the world, to honour and celebrate the Goddess.

In Brigit's Isles there are many wonderful women whose lives are dedicated to the Goddess, who express their love for Her through priestessing, healing, creativity, artwork, writing and in daily life. They include women born in Brigit's Isles and those who have come from other lands to make their homes here. This section includes some of Britain and Ireland's leading Goddess women talking about what the Goddess means to them. They are leading women only in the sense that they are among the first in modern times to stand up for the Goddess, to be seen and heard in an often hostile patriarchal world. They are presented in first name alphabetical order.

Goddess Conference "Wisdom" Banner painted by Willow Roe

Asphodel Long

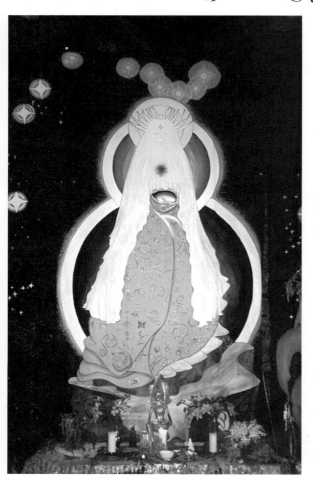

Asphodel Long is often called a Grand Mother of the Goddess movement in Brigit's Isles for her pioneering work in bringing the Goddess back into our consciousness. She is one of a handful of British women who began to explore the Goddess in the 1960's and her work has been an inspiration to many of us who followed after her. She is particularly known for her work with the Matriarchy Study Group, who in the 1970's and 80's explored all kinds of Goddess myths and texts, and for her original book *In a Chariot Drawn by Lions* (Women's Press). She has now retired from active life, but is still writing. She lives at Rye in Sussex.

As a child, I grew up surrounded, in my mind, by goddesses. I must have been about nine years old, when I first encountered them in the pages of The Jewish Encyclopaedia. This set of numerous volumes was one of the few reading resources open to me in a strict Orthodox Jewish household. The others I remember, included biographies of mothers of great Jewish thinkers (such thinkers of course were all men). But it was the notion of the existence of goddesses that inspired me, a lonely and 'difficult ', motherless girl who found the God encountered in the pages of the bible and in the synagogue services both frightening and remote. Here in these books, under headings such as Egyptology, Idolatry, etc., I found Isis, Maat, Asherah, Ashtoreth; and a few years later at school, there were their Greek and Roman sisters Astarte, Aphrodite and Artemis.

Asphodel Long

For all my childhood years until I left school and home at the age of sixteen these goddesses were by me. I was frightened of them, but they were close, not distant and their nearness was a female nearness, and my terrors were of their power, but mediated by their gender. They were like me, of me, but greater by far .

Then I put them out of my mind as I entered work, politics, sexuality, motherhood, the struggle to stay alive in the war and all the rest. I became an atheist, established my position as what was called a 'secular Jew', and agreed with the pundits that religion was the opium of the people. In particular I grew disillusioned with left-wing politics, not least because of its hypocrisy about the equality of women. I looked and fought for a milieu that believed this not to be a sham but a comprehensive reality.

It took over thirty years to find it. There in the London Women's Liberation Movement in 1975 I became part of The Matriarchy Study Group which sought not only to deal with the problems in terms of today's inequalities, but called upon the past to support the thesis that the female had not always been subordinate, but from earliest times had been part of the divine.

The Matriarchy Study Group allied the political with the spiritual, the intellectual with the emotional. We published "Goddess Shrew" in 1977, then "Politics of Matriarchy" and "Menstrual Taboos". These reached out widely (we read them in our women's group in Glastonbury, KJ) and I think became part of the foundation

Goddess Conference 1996: Singing to Mary the Mother Goddess in Glastonbury Abbey

of the women's Goddess movement in this country. The work was continued by the Matriarchy Research and Reclaim Network, which still exists, and publishes regularly.

The Goddess movement has flowered widely and has been influential in many different forms. In addition to the popular dimension, I am specially pleased to note and be a part of the developing action to bring Goddess studies and academe closer. In this, the new(ish) discipline of Feminist Theology can play a large part. There have been some marvellous investigations done by feminist scholars that open up completely new and women-oriented horizons in traditional texts, and also questions asked that amplify our Goddess knowledge.

I have found that academic work enhances our perceptions and our spirituality can enhance our intellectual understanding. Shifting the old parameters of androcentric bigotry to a feminist mode of enquiry opens up an optimistic scene for us. For myself it has been a flowering of my mind and spirit.

I became connected again to the Goddesses of my childhood, as well as to the politics of my adult years. I realised I had found my life's task: to research and to communicate especially to women the fact that there is a different path for us. It has been a marvellous twenty five years. The different parts of my life and being all combined for me, and I have seen a huge development of women's and feminist spirituality flower in that time.

Caitlin Matthews

Caitlin Matthews is a well known and prolific writer, songstress, teacher, shaman and priestess of the Goddess. She is the author of 36 books including *Celtic Devotional* and *Singing the Soul Back Home*. She is co-founder of FiOS, the Foundation for Inspirational and Oracular Studies. She teaches shamanism and the sacred oracular arts throughout the world. Caitlin is married to writer John Matthews with whom she has written amongst other Goddess books: *Ladies of the Lake*. She has a shamanic practice in Oxford.

The earliest Goddess forms that came to me at twilight derived from the chalk downland of my home: featureless mother-forms reminiscent of Stone Age culture. My first rituals back in 1965 were performed in the night-dark woodland; songs and poems of my own, that still come as spontaneous gifts of honouring, echoed then across the chalk downs, My call to priestessing was received here; the later ritual ordination was merely a further unspiralling of this core vocation.

Caitlin Matthews

It is possible to ascertain the nature of someone's spiritual kinship, their association with a deity or spirit, by the gifts a person mediates, for the gifts of the gods shine through the burning glass of the soul. My gifts define the deities who work through me, since every priestess or priest is merely a garment of the divine. My work is the opening of doors, enabling initiation into otherworlds. Through my voice which I have entirely given over to the spirits, the midwifing of the soul is accomplished - sometimes into different aspects of life, sometimes into the release of death. My core dedication is to restore the story of the soul, within the context of its own metaphors, to the primal landscape where spiritual exchange between clients and their inspirational deities or spirits can take place.

My books on the Divine Feminine include "Voices of the Goddess", "Elements of the Goddess" and "Sophia: Goddess of Wisdom, Bride of God", where I have explored respectively my long personal association with the key-holding Rhiannon, the immensity of the Ninefold Inspirers who form the

Goddess in the Cart procession through the rainy streets of Glastonbury to the Tor in 2000 carrying 120 of Lydia Ruyle's Goddess banners

Weaving Goddess and the Wise Goddess of the Excluded. All these forms remain spiritual helpers who initiate my priestessing. In addition I have many Gods and male spirits who guide and assist me.

My deepening dedication to the spirits of the universe has led me to work in a contemporary framework within my own community as a shaman. This has brought great simplicity and immediacy to my service. Bringing the spiritual transaction of the divine to the needs, fragmentation and disharmonies of people, has made me very adaptable to many spiritual traditions. As a spiritual chameleon I really do feel at home wherever the Divine is honoured. As long as spiritual hospitality is extended, this is always possible for me; the spiritual forms can be male or female, it doesn't matter.

The greatest challenge has been to find what clients consider of spiritual importance to themselves, since many younger people have no religious background even to react against, these days. Here I cooperate directly with the animistic nature of the universe to bring any healing or help with the aid of my spiritual helpers. Within everyone's life experience there is always something that inspires and gives them hope: nature, music, friends, animals, By working with these tangible assets it is possible to tap into the client's spiritual currency. Again and again this proves to have sacred form in the otherworlds: sometimes a goddess, a spirit, a god or a mythic animal. The spiritual language of the universe is diverse, symbolic, meaningful and can always be addressed in song.

No boxes, definitions or traditions constrain my priestessing: where there is need, pain, fear or disconnection, that is where I am sent. Only the specific need of the occasion or circumstance defines how I shall work. The spirits who come to assist sometimes stand behind me, sometimes embodying within me. The privilege of briefly becoming the arms, hands and voice of a goddess or of some other spirit is beyond measure.

Those who see any glamour in priestessing or shamanizing do not also see what duties and responsibilities accompany the gifts.

Unless daily communication passes between me and my spiritual inspirers, my service becomes empty and worthless. To be 'on open access' means to have less personal life and comfort. Humanly I do kick against this; maturely I also have to acknowledge its necessity and retire into privacy and silence. There when I am held in balance by the inspiration, encouragement, compassion and wisdom of Wise Ones, the love that supports me becomes the love that I can offer. Praise to them!

To receive details of Caitlin's events, courses and books, and membership of FiOS, contact Caitlin Matthews, BCM Hallowquest, London WC1N 3XX, UK, or consult www.hallowquest.org.uk.

Carolyn Hillyer

Carolyn Hillyer is a original and inspired Goddess-loving artist whose creativity is applied to every area she turns to. She is a wonderful painter, musician and writer who has exhibited, performed and given women's workshops for many years, both within Britain and internationally. She

Carolyn Hillyer playing at the Goddess Conference

has recorded eight albums, four of which are solo works, and has published four books of writings. Her paintings are exhibited as sacred installations and form the centre point to the workshop journeys that she shares with women. Her home and studios are based in an ancient longhouse settlement at the heart of the high wild moor lands of southwest England, where she lives with her two children and her husband, the composer Nigel Shaw, with whom she both writes music and performs concerts. She has travelled with her work to Australia, USA, Russia, the Baltic States and Eastern Europe as well as regularly to Holland and Germany.

My first awakening to a female expression of spirit came during my early twenties and was a natural progression both from my years of involvement in women's political issues and from starting to live more closely with the land, in an isolated rural community where many of

Lau He Raumi: First Hearth. Painting by Carolyn Hillyer

the women worked with moon cycles and earth rites. Digging my feet and hands into the soil brought me quickly to an appreciation of, and absorption in, women's sacred mysteries, which intensified dramatically and suddenly in 1989 when I painted my first large goddess figure. Then the creative gates opened and the images that I had been stowing inside for years began to flood out. At first I painted in a frenzy, using old board, household emulsion, whatever was at hand, and working in a hut so small that I stood outside, exposed to elemental inspiration, and worked on the painting through the open doorway. Gradually I slowed down and the paintings became more focused. My small son and income-generating commercial cartoon work (now happily left far behind) meant that I painted at night and often by candlelight, a habit that after thirteen years I have found hard to kick. I prefer the otherworldliness of night work, the dark spaces where the veils to creative revelation are thin, and even now my studio functions perfectly in an ancient barn with minimal natural light.

My move to Dartmoor in 1991 changed everything. Working with the paintings, and with the women who stepped into them, became a more deeply intense and powerful experience, influenced as they were by the extraordinary landscape around me. Then the women I painted started to sing to me. In 1992 I found my own

Detail of 'Graunig: The Greening' Painting by Carolyn Hillyer

voice and recorded my first album of goddess songs. Since that time the painting, the writing and the singing have woven together into a rich cloth that continues to unfold before me. I am ever grateful to touch the hands of these weavers.

I always exhibit my paintings as sacred shrines. I paint in cycles and circles; councils and gatherings of spirit women who arrive with their own myths and magical viewpoints. I am often surprised by who appears at the end of my brush. I am sometimes tested hard by them. I am always excited by the process of peeling back the layers to see who waits to be revealed, and when I feel that strange tug at the base of my womb, I know that I am getting close.

My inspiration is Dartmoor and the strange bleak beauty of her hills and valleys. On some level these moors run through everything I do. I paint to remember. *I paint to describe the unfathomable nature of the wild land. In a sense I paint landscapes, for each spirit woman is the soul of the land in human form. And each spirit woman can serve to remind us to be brave and wild and free.*

Carolyn can be contacted through the Seventh Wave Music website: www.seventhwavemusic.co.uk

Cheryl Straffon

Cheryl Straffon is best known as a writer living in Cornwall who wrote and published the popular *Pagan Cornwall: Land of the Goddess.* Incarnated this time in 1947 with Sun and Moon in Virgo and Leo rising, she studied English and Comparative Religion at London and Cambridge Universities. In the 1990's she lived and worked on Women's Land in Cornwall, helping to facilitate women's Goddess-celebrating groups. She published *The Earth Goddess - Pagan & Celtic Legacy of the Land* and in 2000 set up *Dor Dama Press* to publish books on the Goddess. Authors so far include Monica Sjoo and Jill Smith. She gave a presentation on British Goddesses at the International Goddess Festival in Santa Cruz and guides Goddess groups to sacred sites in Cornwall. She is currently the coeditor with

Cheryl Straffon

Sheila Bright of the new *Goddess Alive!* magazine. She is working on a new book *In Search of the Goddess.*

In the late 1980s I went on holiday to the Greek island of Lesbos, taking with me a paperback book I had recently come across, entitled "The Goddesses and Gods of Old Europe" by an author called Marija Gimbutas, about whom I knew nothing. But I thought it might be a good book to dip into while I was away, in that kind of desultory way one does on holiday. When we arrived in Lesbos, much to our disgust it rained solidly day and night for the first 3 days. I had nothing else to do but read the book I had bought with me. After 3 days the sun came out, but by then my life was for ever changed. It is no exaggeration to say that Gimbutas' book was the most major influence on me and my life.

Ever since I had been a teenager I had felt there was a spirit in everything, and that in some strange way I did not understand everything in the Universe was connected in some great spider's web. I had no name for it - the Romantic poets and their pantheistic beliefs were the closest I could identify with, and when I got into paganism and ritual in the late 1970s that seemed to give it a structure. But it was Gimbutas book that showed me for the first time that I was not alone in my beliefs in the spirituality of a Mother Earth and a Goddess, and not only 'not alone' but that peoples all over the world had loved, revered and celebrated the Goddess for thousands of years in the past. When I finished that book I felt I had at last come home.

Main altar at Goddess Conference 2000 with stunning backdrop of the Nine Morgens painted by Thalia Brown. Photo: Tony Arihanto

Since then the Goddess has been with me every day and in every way. At times She has been a testing deity, as my life has changed in unexpected and challenging ways. She has been both the healing Bride/Bridgit, and also the tempestuous and destructive Kali, the youthful Artemis and the crone Cailleach.. But She is who I am, and I am a part of Her. She is my Mother Earth, and also the magic of the stars. She has led me to seek Her out in my native Cornwall and all over the world; She has stimulated me into researching and reclaiming Her; and into writing books and articles about Her, and

Priest/esses of Avalon with some of the 120 Goddess banners designed and created by Lydia Ruyle, flying on Glastonbury Tor 2000

giving talks and workshops about Her that have put me into contact with many other wonderful Goddess-celebrating people. She has also led me to a deeper understanding of ritual and the Wheel of the Year through celebrating the festivals in Her honour. And perhaps most of all She has brought another Goddess- celebrating lover and partner into my life with whom I have been able to share Her, learn more about Her and for us to be able to grow and change with Her together.

The Goddess has been my inspiration, my purpose, and the centrifugal force that powers my life. She is my DNA, my deity within and without, and weaves the spiral around which I twist and I turn. She is the matrix of my being, the womb from whence I came and to where I will one day return. On those fateful days on Lesbos Marija Gimbutas helped to change me for ever, and it is the Goddess who continues to lead me to where She needs me to go.

For further information on Cheryl's publications including the new Goddess Alive! magazine contact her at Whitewaves, Boscaswell Village, Pendeen, Penzance Cornwall TR19 7EP

Foosiya Miller

Foosiya (Freddie) Miller is an inspired Goddess sculptor and artist who currently lives in Herefordshire. She has exhibited her artwork each year at the Glastonbury Goddess Conference and for the last three years has created, with help from others, large stunning Goddess statues of the Crone, the Maiden and the Virgin Goddess, for the Conference using willow withies. Her beautiful drawings and paintings illustrate this book.

I was born by the sea, my home a wild and beautiful environment. I have always known my connection with nature, its inherent, instinctual in a child, especially when given the freedom and encouragement to explore. Childhood nurtured in me a love of the natural world. I was fascinated and excited by life. In my youth I recall feeling an intoxicating and sensual effect of its beauty. Art became a way for me to express this sense of beauty, so powerful in me. Being creative heightened and deepened the experience, reaffirmed my connection physically and imaginatively to a reality beyond the superficial.

'Doe & Mother', painting by Foosiya Miller

The process of making an image is a new experience each time, an unknown visioning. Art was my meditation upon, and affirmation of, beauty. I went off to art college at 17 and since then (I'm almost 50 now!), art has been a spiritual focus in my life, a conduit of expression I could not have done without.

Whilst at art college, I had a strong desire to travel, to see the world and other cultures, I felt mainstream Western culture art was the domain of men, like so much else. I travelled extensively, my interest in religion, as

Lammas bread dough shaped into corn plaits and the body of the Goddess on its way to the bakers, Goddess Conference 2000

well as art, took me to Islamic countries, to India and eventually to join a Catholic convent. The religious life suited me completely and I remember those years as being incredibly fruitful and happy. But as fate would have it, my restlessness returned me back again to travel and work amongst refugees in Africa, and to be more politically active.

I first learned about the ancient Goddess religions and the resurgence of interest in earth-centred spirituality through the women's movement and eco-feminism. Books by Merlin Stone, Marija Gimbutas and Susan Griffin, brought everything into focus, revealing all the relevant facts and history omitted from my education. I realised just how much a symbol of empowerment for women the Goddess is and always has been, and how in my own culture images of Her have all but disappeared.

From the earliest times our ancestors have left sacred images of the female form. I began to discover the abundance of art throughout civilisation, that revered the Great Mother as the all-powerful giver of life. The Goddess has been recognised in many manifestations and by many names throughout human history. I discovered her to be a universal image, an immanent force, permanent in the lives and imagination of peoples, both past and present. In my late twenties and early thirties, all this information was a revelation to me, and I have been continually inspired ever since.

I feel that a spiritual revolution must come before a political one; that the malaise that permeates our social fabric and physical environment is due to the domination of people by patriarchal thoughts and monotheistic religions for so long.

As an artist who follows the Goddess tradition, I work to create images that once again honour the female form and symbolise our deep and sacred connection with the Earth and each other. The Goddess has again become a muse for the arts, she is a prime inspiration for many women artists, poets, writers and musicians who seek to restore balance.

Jana Runnalls

Jana Runnalls is a singer, songwriter, recording artist, performer, musician and teacher who lives and works in Glastonbury. Jana was a leading light in the colourful wave of lesbian feminist culture of the 1970/80s as half of the musical duo, *Ova*. They lived in squats, went on *Reclaim the Night* demos, lived the politics of women's empowerment and formed collectives to further the cause. Their music reflected their lives: the passion and struggle, understanding the need for global Sisterhood, for a politics beyond national boundaries to help each other create a more compassionate world. Concern for the environment was part of that and they sang about it all. Performing within a showcase of women's culture, Ova played against the backdrop of Monica Sjoo's painting, *God Giving Birth* in central London in 1977. This was Jana's first experience of the Goddess expressed culturally, politically. It touched a place in her that was seeking for spiritual direction. Jana began visiting sacred sites and singing about her experiences.

My first Goddess song was "Bloodstream" written in 1981 after visiting Avebury and Silbury Hill. It is about the source of the River Kennet:

Jana Runnalls

"Bloodstream growing, bloodstream flowing
Taking me with you into unseen memories
Other worlds, other times
We have lived so many times before"

I continued searching for a more ancient awareness of life through the earth, seasons, trees and plants. Connecting with other Goddess women around Europe and the States, I became tuned in to our collective need to know ourselves from a woman-centred spirituality. I went on to experience the overwhelming energy of women focusing their loving power together at the 'Embrace The Base' demonstration at Greenham Common Airbase. I felt the need to 'name' the magic I felt from Mother Nature, to express how we as women connect to her creatively, beyond the head space of politics, but without abandoning those understandings - where heart tempers head and spirit inspires us to go further, deeper into our sacred nature.

Present Revelations

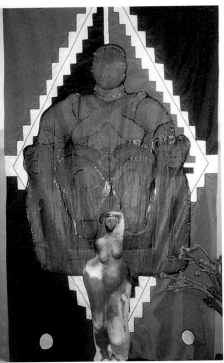

Altar at the Goddess conference with one of Lydia Ruyle's banners behind

My first 'Goddess' album appeared in 1985, called "Ancestral Dream", it explores our collective ancestral memories journeying into the feeling of the ancient Goddesses, such as Tiamat, Kali, Kore and Bride. "We all Come from Goddess" was being sung by women in many cultures at that time, as we reclaimed our matriarchal roots in women's festivals worldwide. My second album, "Eye of the Womb" was recorded all over the U.K. as I travelled from one power spot to another, journeying deep into the dark power of Mother Earth. It was then that I realised that each of my recordings was a "journey" or pilgrimage, searching for my connection to the Source.

After the death of my father and when I came to live in Glastonbury in 1994, the actual concept of 'sacred journey' became clear to me and "Speaking in Tongues" was born. It travels into the underworld to meet with the dark grandmothers, Cerridwyn, Durga and Kali, deep in the crystal caves - facing the death of the old and embracing the light of the new. "Lady of the Lake" (with Katrina Brown) followed in 1997. We travelled out into the lake surrounding the Isle of Avalon at dawn to record the opening parts of the album. The magic is tangible - we became both the pilgrim and the sacred landscape. We travelled through magical gateways, encountering faery people, guides and elementals. It describes the energies of the sacred power spots in Avalon with such chants as "Bloodwell" in Chalice Well, "Gwynn the King" inside the Tor, "Sanctuary" for Bride's Mound and "Sacred Grove" for the ancient Oak Grove in the centre of Avalon:

"Enter into the Sacred Grove of Our Lady
Hear her voice singing in the trees
Ancient Mystery
Circle of oak, circle of stone,
Circle around the fire"

In entering the new millennium we have a much greater awareness of the need for the Goddess in our lives. We have the shared responsibility for bringing balance and wholeness back into a fragmented world. I feel privileged to be living in a community where we are all trying to achieve that one goal.

For information on her music and workshops contact Jana via her website: www.voiceofpower.com
or email: jana.runnalls@virgin.net

Jane Brideson

Jane Brideson is a painter and a witch whose first conscious connection to the Goddess was in the early 1980's when she cast her first circle and did her first ritual. Her paintings: include : The Bringer of Winter, Spirit of the Blackthorn, The Corn Maiden, Drawing Down the Moon, Maiden, Queen and Crone. In progress are Dark Moon Goddess and Full Moon Goddess. Her work has been reproduced on the covers of several magazines including *Pagan Dawn, Wood and Water, New Moon Rising* and in Nancy Passmore's *Lunar Calendar - Dedicated to the Goddess in Her Many Guises*. Illustration work includes the

'Boand', painting by Jane Brideson

Lighting the Lammas Bonfire in Bushey Combe, 1999 Goddess Conference

Beginners Guide series of books on The Goddess, Witchcraft, Paganism etc., and *The Wheel of the Year - Myth and Magic through the Seasons* with Teresa Moorey. She exhibits regularly at The Goddess Conference in Glastonbury and is a member of The British Visionary Artists' Group at the Pagan Federation Annual Conference. She has recently moved to live in Ireland.

How does the Goddess inspire my work and my life? Finding where to start answering this question isn't easy. I could say that my path to the Goddess began in the early 1980's, in London, when I first became involved with feminism, politics and women's issues, when I met my first witch, when I did my first solo ritual but that would be to ignore lighting candles aged 13 to make spells, being overwhelmed by the beauty of Nature and visiting the faeries with my Mother when I was a child. So in retrospect the Goddess has always been in my life even though I could not name Her.

Over the years I have opened to Her, learned more about Her and experienced Her presence in ritual so strongly that I've wept with joy. She is the one that I worship, that I turn to for comfort and help, that I get angry with when my life doesn't go 'right'. It is the Goddess that I see in the land, the turning of the year and the changing Moon. She empowers me and it is She who inspires my work.

In 1993 I began uniting my love of the Goddess, my Craft (I am a witch) and my work by painting a set of cards depicting the Moon's phases as a focus for ritual. Three years on at Imbolc I made the decision to leave my job and dedicate my life to Her, earning my living by painting, selling cards and prints through my company, Dark Moon Designs.

My work has naturally fallen into two categories, the more graphic images such as: celebrations of the festivals, an annual Lunar Calendar etc., and the Goddess paintings. My first series of paintings were a response to seeing the Goddess and womens' lives reflected in the changing seasons. These are: The Changing Seasons of the Goddess - Seed Woman, Spring Maiden, Green Woman, Copper Woman and Hedgerow Crone.

As I researched more into our native Goddesses I started to work with them in ritual using pathworking, dream images and invocation. From there I began painting a series of British Goddesses, the first of which was Blodeuwedd, who came to me so clearly at Spring Equinox. My intention is to paint not only the better known Goddesses such as Bride and the lesser known, Sadb for example, but to eventually portray the Goddesses who are hinted at in obscure texts and pieces of poetry and folklore, those who have been sleeping and are yet to return to our consciousness.

This has become my life time's task as with each painting I complete I discover other 'aspects' to each Goddess and therefore new images to explore. The British Goddess paintings completed so far include: Arianrhod, Blodeuwedd, Boand, Bride, Cerridwen, Sadb, the Morrigan, and Rhiannon.

I would like to take this opportunity to acknowledge the women that have helped me along my path either through their books, through shared ritual or through friendship: Carolyn Hillyer, Doreen Valiente, Kathy Jones, Leisel Silverstone, Lou Hart, Shan Jayran, Shekinah Mountainwater, Starhawk and Teresa Moorey. Blessed be.

For more information about Jane's work please contact Dark Moon Designs, Rainbow Cottage, Clandaff, Rosemallin, Co Laois, Ireland. Email: morrigan@mac.com

Jill Smith

Jill Smith was born in London 1942, studied acting at RADA in 1960- '61, became Jill Bruce, played roles; had 3 children, worked as a cleaner and Market Researcher '67- '74; worked in Community Art with family in early '70's, became Performance Art duo with Bruce Lacey '74- '82. After Science Fantasy productions, suddenly she 'awoke' into Earth Mysteries and for several years performed extravagant

'Wise Crone of the Winter Mound' by Jill Smith

ceremonial, celebratory, cyclic rituals at Fayres, Festivals, Art Colleges, Galleries etc. She had two major exhibitions: at Acme Gallery and the Serpentine. Then came Goddess.

Her books: include *The Callanish Dance*, Capall Bann, *Mother of the Isles*, dor dama Press. She has made contributions to anthologies:: *The Sun is the East*, R.B. Photographic, *The Best of Resurgence*, John Button (Ed) Green Books, *Earth Walking Sky Dancers*, Leila Castle (Ed) Frog, *In the Footsteps of the Goddess'* Cristina Biaggi (Ed) Kit .

Present Revelations

Goddess came into my life, enfolded me into her reality, in the late '70's early 80's. I learned not from others or from books, but as though I were called, like an erring daughter, back to something of which I had been part millennia and lifetimes before, but had forgotten. It was a 're-membering', a transmission from place, cycles of nature, sun, moon and everything.

I experience her as 'Goddess' rather than 'The Goddess'. She is an indefinable, all-encompassing energy, with me all the time and part of everything I do, the very energy of Creation and power of every aspect of Nature. Sometimes there are very specific energies connected to certain places or times of year which I feel I know in a very personal way, like friends or companions and who I experience as 'beings' rather than 'goddesses'. Allowing me to receive transmission of their lineages, these are also with me at all time - inspiring, comforting, teaching and challenging.

In 1982 I left everything and went out into the landscape, staying for days and nights at sacred sites, honouring the spirits I encounters. I made extensive journeys through the land, lying to sleep on the earth each night like a child nestling into its mother's body, comforted and protected. I began to externalise my experience in pastel pictures and into poetry which I would perform with slides of the images. It always seemed that Goddess energy and the spirits of place would pour forth through the pictures rather than I being responsible for creating them.

With my fourth child I lived in the Western Isles of Scotland ('86- '96) where the energy of Goddess was most powerful and potent. I met her as Brighde, the ancient spirit of the Islands themselves; in the ancestral Grandmothers whose energy still inhabits the Callanish stones; in the extraordinary presence of 'The Sleeping Beauty' woman-mountain who gives birth to the moon every 19 years and I encountered her in the awesome energy of the 'Cailleach Bheure' - Creation Ancestress and Goddess of Winter.

I am resting a while in the soft rounded greenness of Glastonbury, gently sustained by the Goddess energy which streams forth from her landscape, and am especially inspired by the Chalice Well - her ever-flowing lifeblood. These spirits and beings as well as those of the Hebrides, continue to flow through my work and the experience of 'now' merges with that of a very ancient past.

For more information on Jill's work contact her at 20 Monington Rd., Glastonbury, Somerset, BA6 8HE

Julie Felix

Julie Felix is an international singer/songwriter whose career began with the protest songs of the 1960's and 70's continuing on into Goddess songs in the 90's and 00's. For several years she has brought large groups of women on pilgrimage to the sacred sites of Britain and Ireland and she is regular performer at the Glastonbury Goddess Conference delighting audiences with her singing and encouraging us all to chant our hearts out for the Goddess.. Her numerous CDs include *Fire - My Spirit* which includes Goddess songs. Julie lives in Hertfordshire but spends much of the year travelling and singing around the world.

Julie Felix singing at Glastonbury Goddess Conference with Lydia Lite on drums. Photo by Tony Arihanto

Like so many of my Goddess sisters, I feel She has always been in my heart. It took a while for Her to manifest in my conscious mind. After all She and I had walls of Catholicism and Patriarchy to break through. I think the key to welcoming the Goddess into my conscious heart came when I began visiting Her sacred sites: the Merry Maidens, Boscawen-un and Madron's Well in Cornwall, the Tor and Chalice Well in Glastonbury, New Grange in Ireland, and oh, so many magical places throughout the British Isles. The powerful energy I experienced at these places made the Goddess and Her presence so very real to me; not just an idea in my Geminian mind.

Chanting, singing and creating rituals at these sacred sites re awoke in me a deep sense of wonder and adventure I had known as a child. Also it made me aware of my need to express reverence. With this conscious connection with the Divine, in myself as well as in the world around me, my music and performances took on another dimension. I seem to be able to use my voice more expressively, and play my guitar with more confidence. The Goddess tours I've led, and my participation in The Goddess Conference have been beacons or flood lights on my path, and helped to deepen my awareness and affection for She who is all knowing, all loving, and ever present. All Blessings Be!!!

For information about Julie's recordings and current performances contact Remarkable Records Tel. 01 923 284413

Katheryn Trenshaw

Katheryn Trenshaw is a fine artist and an experienced facilitator of circles specialising in healing through art, ritual, body awareness and creativity. Her contagious passion for life and her ability to encourage celebration and making the everyday sacred are hallmarks of her workshops and exhibitions. Her *Affirming the Female Body* and *Drawing Down the Moon* groups for women as well as the *Celebrating the Body* camp for men and women take place in the UK, Europe and the US. Katheryn's watercolors and raku-fired sculptures are displayed in galleries from California to Leiden.

'Sticks and Stones and Ancient Bones', painting by Katheryn Trenshaw.

I have always been a creatress/artist from the time I got the hang of the opposable thumb. I am an artist. I don't think of myself as a Goddess artist! I am, however, a woman increasingly in touch with my own divinity…and the closest thing to naming that is the Goddess. I feel a contemporary connection to ancient wisdom. And so, here are some questions I find myself pondering: Who is the goddess to me? Where does she live? How does she speak to me?

The divine feminine has crept in to my life gradually and steadily ever since I can remember. She midwives my art and every act of creation. Both birther and midwife, I

Painting 'Birthing Transformation', by Katheryn Trenshaw

have come to know her in many guises. When I surrendered to the deeply personal and sacred in my life - the dark, moist places where the Goddess lives - my work moved into the realm of the mythical. At a certain point I stopped caring about making aesthetically beautiful or culturally pleasing images; I went for the more gutsy, soulful and untamed. Art-making allowed me access to dangerous and frightening realms - my inner self - and my work became my autobiography.

When I created the 'Breaking the Silence' exhibition in 1990 (a series of nearly 100 sculpted masks and paintings to encapsulate the varied emotions that are experienced in the healing process from child sexual abuse that toured throughout the US and parts of Europe) I was beginning to re-member myself and my divinity. Out of pain and chaos, I was putting the pieces back together. I was remembering the Goddess within and coming to know her face.

She lives in my belly and at the core of my cellular memory. How could I create something not connected to myself, my body, my divinity, the Goddess? At best, she inspires me to create the most juicy work…raw and visceral while still well crafted and formed. This is my favourite dialogue with the Goddess. It goes something like, "OK, I'll be your muse, your mother, sister, lover, and all you need to do is get out of your own way and allow images to arise out of the belly. Give form to the ineffable. Then share and teach the same with your heart wide open." The liberating thing about the Goddess, for me, is reconnecting and remembering being juicy and wild. Over time voluptuous women/goddesses simply became integral to my work.

As my life changes, I ask for different qualities to come into it. In the last decade, I have chosen a goddess/archetype that holds qualities with which I would like to be imbued to be my guide for each year. I 'research' her, dance her and collect images of her. I paint her and write songs about her. This practice has become a part of the Drawing Down the Moon yearlong group I lead. It is powerful to have a subcommittee of goddesses to a circle of wonderful women! The Goddesses invoked have a huge impact on the shape of the year for each circle. It is potent magic. And, though it may sound simple, like the descent of Inanna it is sometimes the most challenging journey of all.

I see the Goddess in every woman. I relish the diversity that I am privileged to witness in my travels, my community and in circles of women I participate in and lead. I celebrate the gorgeousness of the Goddess beneath rolls of fat and anorexia, behind scars and illness, in creative genius and graceful gestures. I find the Goddess in the sacred sites and stone circles that inspire my work most profoundly. But equally I find her in the mundane everyday acts of life...right down to preparing meals, simple acts of kindness, gardening and cleaning.

So, I am not a goddess artist, but there is a passion in me to create, to celebrate life, to re-member. Every act of creation is an act of the goddess. May we all be inspired to create, celebrate and re-member our most vibrant and alive selves

Information about Katheryn's workshops and artwork may be found through www.ktrenshaw.com or post@ktrenshaw.com Tel. +44 (0)1803 863552 POBox 3, Totnes, Devon TQ9 5WJ England

The Goddess's Face formed out of fruit at the Conference Fruit Feast

Monica Sjoo

Monica Sjoo is a pioneering Goddess artist whose beautiful original paintings have inspired Goddess seekers for over thirty years. Unrecognised by the establishment artworld, her unique paintings are themselves inspired by visions and dreams received at ancient sacred sites all over Brigit's Isles, Europe and Scandinavia, blending ancient meanings with modern expressions. Monica is also a writer who has contributed thought-provoking feminist articles to many journals and anthologies. Her books, include *The Great Cosmic Mother,* (Harper Row), coauthored with Barbara Mor, *Return of the Dark/Light Mother or New Age and Armageddon* (Plain View Press.), and *The Norse Goddess* (Dor Dama Press). She lives and works in Bristol and travels widely, speaking and exhibiting her paintings .

'Earth Our Mother',
one of Monica Sjoo's
early Goddess paintings
from 1984.

Without my belief in the Goddess I wouldn't be alive today, because what is happening in the world is so awful. It's only my awareness of that eternal spiritual world of the Earth, being able to tune into that Source, which keeps me sane. Sacred Earth is reality, not the patriarchal unreality which has made the world so ugly, but they cannot destroy the Earth.

Before the women's movement began I felt ancient women speaking through me. I was a link in a great chain of women going back through time. I always had a sense of being communicated with in dreams. I painted my first Goddess painting 'God Giving Birth' in 1968, based on my experience of giving birth at home, when I felt the power in my own body. I had a vision of light intermixing with a velvety blackness, creating an incredibly luminous darkness. I didn't name this at the time as Goddess but that's what it was. I'm sure that this is how the ancient neolithic people saw Her, as a great indwelling power, as Earth and Cosmos, but not personalised.

In 1963 I read Robert Graves The White Goddess. I had no idea until then that there had been Goddess cultures and it blew my mind. I began a 20 year journey of exploration researching every obscure reference. This formed the basis for The Great Cosmic Mother which was first published in 1981.

In 1978 while taking mushrooms at Silbury Hill near Avebury I experienced the Earth as truly alive, Silbury being the pregnant womb of the Earth. I knew then how She is suffering now as She is abused and raped. I saw the earth moving, undulating, breathing. During the early 80's while living in Wales I began to experience the Goddess in particular forms, as Brigit, Keridwen and Rhiannon. I painted their images as I experienced Her at sacred places. I don't fantasise things. Something usually hits me in the face and makes me see.

In 1985 when my son Leif was killed in a car accident, I experienced flying with him into a great light, which set me on another search trying to understand. Then my eldest son Sean died in 1987 from lymphoma.

I didn't see the ancient women as such until about five years ago. I was at Rainbow Village in the mountains above Orgiva in Andalucia recovering from an operation for a burst appendix. There were too many male images there and they were singing God songs. I had a confrontation with a couple of the men. I was screaming and crying in a tipi, feeling very upset and exhausted. I have been attacked for years, for being too powerful, too tall, too strong, a woman, you name it. A healer gave me some healing and in my mind's eye I saw myself surrounded by a group of ancient multiracial women wearing long gowns and tall headdresses. I saw next to me an African woman with a large lined face. I heard the words,

"Are there great female beings out there waiting for us to be free?"

The healer sensed them too as a great blast of light and energy. These were the women who had communicated with me over the years. Sometime later I had a realisation that I was one of the ancient sisterhood who had returned. I have always felt presences in my paintings and believe that they are gateways to other worlds. My paintings are important messengers and need to be seen.

My life has been extraordinary, a shamanic ordeal which has made me see things in a different way. I believe that unless women rise and the Goddess returns, we will all die.

Lady Olivia Durdin Robertson

Lady Olivia calling in the Goddess at the Goddess Conference

Lady Olivia is the founder with her brother Lawrence Durdin Robertson of the international Fellowship of Isis, a worldwide congregation of Goddess worshipping peoples. Based in a love for the Egyptian Goddess Isis, She of Ten Thousand Names, the Fellowship welcomes all who love the Goddess no matter what particular path they follow. Lady Olivia is a regular presenter at the Goddess Conference and lives at Enniscorthy in southern Ireland.

Goddesses exist. They love. They think. They intervene. And surely this must be so. Can humans be the last expression of manifested Deity?

My first experience of the Goddess came in February 1947. She was a Being more advanced than any human I had ever met - yet in our home we met famous thinkers like Yeats and visited the sage AE. What the difference was I immediately noticed. The Lady's mind was far beyond ours. Compared with Hers, our thoughts are those of a child of five. Her body was made of crystalized light. She had the dignity of a Queen, the power of an athlete and the grace of a dance. Her dress was made of V shapes in violet and green. She visited me in our lovely Slaney valley from a small craft that itself emanated from a mighty spaceship, which I described in my mind as "big as the Queen Mary" - (ship). I was 29 years old.

My second experience of a Goddess came after I had been deeply upset about cruelty to a cat - which I had reported. Below the depths of sleep, within the heart of the earth, I saw a Goddess with long wavy hair made of pure gold light, wearing a long cloak of turquoise blue edged with gold embroidery. She gave me a sense of divine happiness, the like of which I had never known. This was in 1952, in spring. Later She gave Her Name as Dana.

Lady Olivia blessing the Grael of Reverend Celia Thomas in her Lyceum in Street.

My third Visitation from a Goddess came on the 26th September 2000 when I was 83. On the longest day, 22nd June, in bed, I had seen a sun at midnight, preceded by a flash of a white star. On the 6th of September following this, this sun entered my body in the darkness of night - and twice I felt the White Star in my hand.

I was given a vision of the Goddess who presided over this spiritual alchemy on the 26th September 2000. I saw a woman luminous and pale, with hair cut strangely, liquid gold cut in very large petals, short and framing Her face. She wore a white angel dress lighted partly with gold. On my right (Her left), was a very large column, transparent, within which were spirals of dancing motes of gold with a few red and blue 'atoms'. She appeared to be creating this phenomena with a rod, with which She was striking a pendant long crystal. It made an exquisite long drawn sound, fairly high, possibly a top "G". I was wide awake though in bed at dawn, and heard this loud and clear!

Later an Alchemist in California told me others had seen this Goddess and commented on her "hair cut in hearts". She never speaks. Her Name, they said, is BRIGIT. I feel their message for this article is this: "We are above: we are below. We are within yourselves".

The Fellowship of Isis can be contacted at Clonegal Castle, Enniscorthy, Eire. Send a stamped sae for information..

Phillipa Bowers

A selection of Phillipa Bowers sculptures with "Source", one of her most well known images, in the centre

It was Phillipa Bowers' modern day sculptures which first brought the Goddess to life for many women. Whilst a mature student in the sculpture department at West Surrey College of Art and Design Phillipa took some clay home to play with in the holidays and literally allowed it to take whatever form it wished. She had no idea that the shapes which emerged had any historical background and was astonished when a sympathetic tutor told her of their significance. Among the distinctive features of her sculptures were large thighs and hollow bellies filled with poetry, crystals and candlelight. Phillipa lived for many years at Wookey Hole near to the Cave of the famous Witch. She now lives in Cornwall with her partner, painting and writing Goddess novels.

I believe that many of the sculptures I have made were influenced by images from a memory-bank created by our ancestors long ago. I have never knowingly made an exact replica of an ancient figurine or sculpture, preferring inspiration by, rather

than imitation of, the source material.

The joy I felt in 1979 when first I allowed the clay to form the shape it desired within my hands was redoubled on learning that these small rounded female shapes were reminiscent of archaeological

Painting of the 'Birthing Cave' by Phillipa Bowers

specimens found all over the world. The discovery of these goddesses, or votive offerings, Venus figurines and fertility symbols as they have been variously dubbed by archaeologists, was a twofold revelation. Firstly, on finding the round and generous female form celebrated so beautifully helped me understand that I lived in a two-dimensional world lacking depth. Although we have made some progress in our small corner of the planet since then, there are many injustices and imbalances to be put right before one could say that the feminine principle is respected equally with the male in both our society and the world at last.

The second important finding was I felt, and still feel, that through their creations, the people who made the Goddesses continue to communicate their reverence for the earth that nurtured them and their belief that it is a living being as sentient and sensitive as themselves.

Maiden Goddess 2000 with ribbons flying in the wind being carried on Glastonbury Tor by Tony Eagleheart, Kevin Redpath & others

From that time I saw the world in a different light and the creative force that then began to flow through my heart and hands continues to excite and astonish me. I love to paint the spirits inhabiting rocks and trees and the sculptured figures with which nature has adorned the cliffs in this windy corner of Cornish paradise. Whilst living in Wookey Hole I became interested in the Wise Women who were the herbalists, healers and midwives of their communities and I am currently writing a romantic saga about their descendants in the twentieth and twenty-first centuries.

I have no idea where the path of the Goddess might lead me from here; I can only say that it has been a most delightful three-dimensional, adventure getting thus far.

Phillipa's sculptures are available from Starchild, 2-4 High St., Glastonbury , Somerset, BA6 9DU

Rose Flint

After Rose's first early meeting with the Shining Lady she did not *see* her again until she was an adult. She then experienced a visitation from her which utterly changed my life. Rose began to study mythology, particularly Celtic and took a course in *'Women's Mysteries*, closely followed by a short apprenticeship in a shamanistic Native American tradition. She trained as a Priestess of Avalon in 2000 and now offers ceremonies, healing and reading. She is a poet and artist and teaches creative writing and works as an Art Therapist which takes her into a wide variety of health settings. Her poetry has been widely published in magazines and anthologies and her first collection is *Blue Horse of Morning* (Seren).

Rose Flint

"The child curled in the bed waking sleep-drowned into a strangeness of misty light — a shining woman who leans forward for the space of a breath and smiles. And the child knows she has never seen anything more beautiful nor ever been so loved."

I was about five years old at the time. I remember getting out of bed and padding down the corridor to my parents' room to tell them that I had see the 'Virgin Mary.' I couldn't think of any other name for her as I knew nothing else that could explain the light, although she wasn't like any of the images I had seen. My parents were gentle but unimpressed and sent me back to bed. Of course, they told me it was just a dream.

Years later I remembered that I had also called her the Shining Lady. And sometimes, now, I see Her like that - very tall and with a grace that opens my heart so that I remember how to be a child again, and how to see the astonishing reality of the world. She is one of the Shining Ones, her presence is the grace of light in the land, especially the between-time magical light of dawn and twilight, but also moonlight, starlight, February snow-light, all light that is slant and wild and wakes me out of the sleep of my ordinary dulled perception.

I call to many Goddesses now, to Morgan le Fey and her sisters deep in Glastonbury Tor, to Bridget, Lady of the Fires, Fiery Arrow, to Arianrhod of the Silver Wheel and to many others. They are rich and varied their moods and purposes as separate as strands of weather,

Priestesses of Avalon Rachel Houghton, Onya Dowling (with baby) and Ren Chapman calling in the Goddess on top of Glastonbury Tor

yet somewhere in each of them I still find that shiningness: Lady.

Lady is the Lady of the Land. She is the deep connection with the animals and plants. She is Love that connects us to each other. On the rainbow bridge of Her light we may travel between the worlds to bring back the gifts of poetry or healing, beauty or prophecy. She is the swan feather and the fire, she is Mother and vivid Sister. She is Night and owls and Crone wisdom that comes so hard. It is the Lady that ties the lamp to the mast when you make the night sea journey; and she is Ocean, deep, dangerous and dark. In her paradox she holds me in my duality, makes me look at what is real, not only that which can be seen.

Just a dream...We can dream-in how we want our world to be. We can dream-in grace, the shiningness of the Goddess walking in the land: honoured, recognised and loved. And we don't have to close our eyes but simply open them and wake up.

SLEEPING AND WAKING

Some women walk the old paths in their midnight sleep
and sleepwalk through their daily trades
and their romances, deal with their hand-to-mouth monies
as if they were only ephemerals drifting past.
I know a woman who sleepwalks all the hours of her house
only waking when Wind comes from the West to take her
out of the skin of her this-world self.
Wind traces the spine of that self down her back
and the old self-skin falls like a cut coat
onto the bedroom floor as she walks away

through blossomed orchards and groves
of mossy oaks wide as gateways. Wind
rounding her ankles like a spaniel, lifting her hair
like a lover wanting the sweet nape of her neck

she is awake then: to leaves susurration, their groaning
onto the quiet shoulders of rock, rock's monosyllabic answer.
She is awake to each plant's whitelight energy
streaming out of its stalk as she questions voices of water.
Horses follow her in friendship over fields where stars settle
hissing like snakes and white birds fly up in a snow
to tag the streamers of her spirit as she walks.
She is awake to her blood's fume and flow
and the needs of women for moonlight, as she begins
finding rituals again, waking the old paths in her wisdom:
making the healing prayer, the praisesong, the invocation.

Tyna Redpath

Tyna Redpath is the creative owner of the Goddess and Green Man shop in Glastonbury, one of the few shops in Brigit's Isles dedicated to the Goddess and Her consort. She is co-organiser of the Glastonbury Goddess Conference and amongst other work focuses the Womanspirit

Participants in the first Glastonbury Goddess Conference in 1996 with the Lammas Goddess.

Tyna on the right with Kathy at the Goddess Gala Banquet and Masque.

Art exhibitions at the Conference. Tyna is a woman of many talents and is a gifted craftswoman. She lives in Glastonbury with her family.

When I first came to live in Glastonbury almost 20 years ago I was extremely uncomfortable when I became aware that there were women who worshipped the Goddess. What a nonsense! For hadn't I been trained in a rather select Western Mystery School tradition which I was deeply involved in, and I knew this Goddess had no part in it whatsoever? And everyone knows that God is a man, a bloke, a chap, and certainly not a woman! I did my best to ignore this Goddess faction, and would studiously cross the road rather than encounter one of these mistaken women.

My transition and personal transformation took place in 1986, on a sacred journey to the Royal Andes, on the edges of Lake Titicaca in Bolivia. Why should I have been gifted with such a romantic place to meet the Goddess? Because some of us are slow and resistant, and I needed a good hard clobbering! She changes everything she touches.... And I needed to change.

On a beautiful sunset evening Kevin, my partner, and I, decided to make the Christian pilgrimage up a sacred mountain at Copacabana. I stopped at the first 'station of the cross' to make my dedication, calling upon the image of the Christ. I got much more than I bargained for. For instead of Him, I got Her. I was devastated, the margins of my accepted reality shook and disintegrated forever.

Present Revelations

I do not have visions. The true insights I have had direct from Spirit I can still count on the fingers of one hand. But when I do, I know. And have no choice.

She came and plucked me for Her own, and I totally surrendered. By the time we had returned from the top of the mountain, my whole life and consciousness had flipped over completely. And I was in love. With Her. To discover that God is a woman remains the single most shatteringly transformative moment of my life. Everything I held dear and precious was up for grabs - everything was different! And how my soul danced and basked in the forbidden fruit of knowing that I, yes me, and all women, are made in the Image of Goddess. And continues to be so. What a fabulous, glorious, piece of knowing!!! I know I am totally accepted into Her arms, with all my imperfection I am loved. Within that wonderful security I am totally responsible for my life and actions. It ain't easy, it is a hugely challenging and ongoing journey searching for and defining a Goddess centred life and living it. Being true. But I came home and have stayed there.

The Goddess & Green Man shop is at 17 High St., Glastonbury, Somerset, BA6 9DP. Email goddess.shop@uk.com

Tyna in the centre foreground joining in the singing with Julie Felix

Present Revelations

The Glastonbury Goddess Conference

At the time of writing the annual Glastonbury Goddess Conference which is held each Lammastide is the biggest Goddess event in Brigit's Isles. Co-founded and organised by Kathy Jones and Tyna Redpath the

Frederika Hall's fabulous Goddess Dragon Tiamat leads the Maiden Goddess up Glastonbury Tor in 2000

Conference is an abundant cornucopia of ceremonies, talks, workshops, performances, beautiful exhibitions of Womanspirit artwork, stalls, fun, conversation, music, song and dance, all dedicated to the Goddess. There are Circles of Thirteen for support and discussions, a ceremonial Lammas Bonfire, a special Labrynth Ceremony, Gala Buffet and Masque and a Goddess in the Cart procession through the streets of Glastonbury to Chalice Well and the White Spring and on to a Fruit Feast on top of Glastonbury Tor. This procession remembers an ancient tradition of taking the Goddess out from Her Temple through the streets of the town so that the people can adore Her. Each year there are variations in a full programme giving participants an experience of the many faces of the Goddess and the Mysteries of Avalon.

Above: Conference participants bathing in the Vesica Pisces pool at Chalice Well
Below: Women from the Avalonian Free State Choir singing at the Goddess Banquet in 1996

Present Revelations

We invite women and men from all over the world to come to Glastonbury to join with us in celebrating the living presence of the Goddess at Her festival of Lammas, creating create an open loving space in which we can all experience Her. The Goddess Conference is one of the few places in Brigit's Isles where Goddess creativity is openly available on a grand scale and our aim is to encourage British and Irish women to present their work within a friendly, Goddess-loving atmosphere. We also ask selected women from abroad with particular Goddess interests and connections to Glastonbury to present their ideas at the Conference.

If you would like further information contact:
The Goddess Conference, 2-4 High St., Glastonbury, Somerset, BA6 9DU, UK.
Visit our website *http://www.goddessconference.com*
Email <goddessconference@ukonline.co.uk>

The Glastonbury Goddess Temple

In 1999 a group of Goddess-loving people came together, each bringing their own visions, skills and energy in a commitment to create a permanent contemporary Goddess Temple in Glastonbury. We have been raising funds, gathering interested people and building energy. During the past eighteen months we have created beautiful temporary Goddess Temples to celebrate the eight festivals of the year, holding public ceremonies and opening the space for several days to all who wish to explore their relationship to the Goddess.

Our vision is to create a Temple openly dedicated to the Goddess in Glastonbury, a place for celebration and exploration of the divine feminine. It is to be a sacred space, open to all, where our love for Her is welcomed and where we can worship and honour Her in ways that are old and new. We are particularly honouring those Goddesses who are associated with the Isle of Avalon, the Otherworldly counterpart of Glastonbury.

Avalon is a magical land where the Goddess has lived from time immemorial and still lives today. It is a place of birth, healing, transformation, death and rebirth, where we can let go of the old and assist in birthing the new. The Goddesses particularly connected to Avalon are by name - Our Lady of Avalon, She who is Brigit MorgAna; Bridie, Maiden Goddess of Fire; Rhiannon of the Hollow Hills; Madron the Great Mother; Tyronoe the Crone of Avalon; the Nine Morgens including

Morgen La Fey; Our Lady Mary of Glastonbury; Tor Goddess; Lady of the Lake; and Lady of the Holy Springs and Wells.

We are sounding a note, calling to Goddess-loving people to support this great project to rebuild Her Temple of Avalon here in Glastonbury. In summer 2001 we found space to rent in the centre of Glastonbury which we will open as permanent Goddess Temple in 2002. If you would like to support this project and for further information please contact:: *The Goddess Temple, 2-4 High St., Glastonbury, Somerset, BA6 9DU, UK*

Brigantia's Autumn Equinox Goddess Temple 2001, laid out with the body of the Goddess on the Temple floor

References and Reading for Inspiration

Spinning the Wheel of Ana, Kathy Jones, Ariadne Publications
The Goddess in Glastonbury, Kathy Jones, Ariadne Publications
In the Nature of Avalon, Kathy Jones, Ariadne Publications
On Finding Treasure, Kathy Jones, Ariadne Publications

The Avebury Cycle, Michael Dames, Thames & Hudson
The Celtic Realms, M Dillon & N Chadwick, Cardinal
The Civilisation of the Goddess, Marija Gimbutas, Thames & Hudson
Complete Irish Mythology by Lady Gregory, The Slaney Press;
Eclipse of the Sun, Janet McCrickard, Gothic Image
A Field Guide to the Little People, Nancy Arrowsmith, Macmillan
The Golden Key and the Green Life, Elizabeth Sutherland, Constable
The Great Cosmic Mother, Monica Sjoo & Barbara Mor, Harper Row
The Herbal Remedies of the Physicians of Myddfai, ed Dr Derek Bryce
Iona, Fiona Macleod, Floris Books;
Irish Mythology Michael Dames, Thames & Hudson
The Island of the Mighty, Evangeline Walton, Pan Books
Kali the Feminine Force, Ajit Mookerjee, Thames & Hudson
Lady of the Beasts, Buffie Johnson, Harper Collins
The Language of the Goddess, Marija Gimbutas, Thames & Hudson
Ladies of the Lake, Caitlin and John Matthews, Aquarian Press
The Mabinogion translated by Lady Charlotte Guest, Dent
The Modern Antiquarian by Julian Cope, Thorsons
Mythic Ireland Michael Dames, Thames and Hudson
New Light on the Stones of Callanish, Margaret & Gerald Ponting
Ortho Nan Gaidheal, Alexander Carmichael, SAP
Pagan Cornwall, Cheryl Straffon, Meyn Mamvro
The Secrets of the Avebury Stones, Terence Meaden, Souvenir Press
The Serpent and the Goddess, Mary Condren, Harper & Row
The Sheela-na-Gigs of Ireland and Britain, Joanne McMahon & Jack Roberts, Mercier Press
The Silbury Treasure Michael Dames, London
Star Names, Their Lore and Meaning, RH Allen, Dover
The Sun and the Serpent, Miller & Broadhurst, Pendragon Press
Troiedd Ynys Prydein, ed. Rachel Bromwich, University of Wales
The White Goddess, Robert Graves, Faber
Women's Encyclopedia of Myths & Secrets, Barbara Walker, Harper Row

Index

Ariadne Publications

Books by Kathy Jones:

Chiron in Labrys: An Introduction to Esoteric Soul Healing

A book about transformation and the healing of disease in the patient and the wounded helaer within the context of the natural cycles and energies of our Mother Earth. A reworking of Alice Bailey's classic teachings on Esoteric Healing based on Kathy's 25 years healing experience.

212pp bk illust.   2001   £11.95

In the Nature of Avalon :
Goddess Pilgrimages in Glastonbury's Sacred Landscape

Beautifully illustrated Goddess pilgrimages in Glastonbury's sacred landscape providing an excellent guide for those who wish to journey through the Veil into the magical Otherworld of the Isle of Avalon. With detailed route directions, maps, Goddess historical and mythic information, and suggestions for prayers , rituals and visualisations all designed to bring you into closer contact with the Goddess.

224pp pbk illust.   2000   £9.99

Breast Cancer: Hanging on by a Red Thread

A strong story based on diary extracts of Kathy's journey through the experience of having breast cancer, looking at the physical, emotional and spiritual aspects of this dangerous disease. With ideas on how to help yourself.

124pp pbk illust.   1998   £8.95

On Finding Treasure: Mystery Plays of the Goddess

An exciting autobiographical account of the transformative work of Ariadne Productions which regularly presents original sacred dramas in Glastonbury. Includes five performed playscripts.

264pp pbk illust.   1996   £9.99

Spinning the Wheel of Ana by Kathy Jones

A spiritual journey to reconnect with the Primal Ancestors of the British Isles, examining the earliest myths and legends and bringing their meaning into the present to create the Ancestral Medicine Wheel of Ana the Great One, ancient Goddess of the British Isles.

262pp pbk illust.   1994   £11.95

Order from Ariadne Publications, 61 Tor View Avenue, Glastonbury, BA6 8AG, Somerset, UK. Wholesale prices available.
Website http://www.kathyjones.co.uk

In the Heart of the Goddess
Train with Kathy Jones
to be a Priestess or Priest of Avalon

Stunning costume for the Priestess of the North, of the Air and Winter created for the Goddess Conference by Cherie Barstow.

Many women and men are called by the mystery of the Isle of Avalon. In particular we are drawn to the memory of the Priestesses of Avalon who were devoted to the Lady, living and working their magic beyond the mists in the sacred land of Avalon. Many have read Marian Zimmer Bradley's wonderful novel *The Mists of Avalon* and felt that longing in the heart to become once again a Priestess of Avalon.

You can now participate in one and four year trainings with the author, Kathy Jones, to become Self-initiated as Priest/ess of Avalon, dedicated to love and serve the Goddess of this sacred land. Successful participants are Self-initiated through the empowerment of their own Souls in a special ceremony at the end of the first year of training. In the following years students enter more deeply into the Mysteries of Avalon and are trained to conduct ceremonies and initiate others into Her Mysteries.

The first year training consists of Nine Circles of the Goddess which take place throughout the year, exploring the teachings and ceremonies connected to the cycles and seasons of the Goddess. Teachings are grounded in Britannia's Sacred Wheel described in this book and earlier in *Spinning the Wheel of Ana* (Ariadne Publications).

If you would like to know more about this training please contact:
Isle of Avalon Foundation, 2-4 High St., Glastonbury, Somerset, BA6 9DU, UK Tel 01458 833933 http://www.isleofavalonfoundation.com